ISO14031: A practical guide to developing environment performance indicators for your business

David Wathey and Mark O'Reilly

London: The Stationery Office

Applications for reproduction should be made in writing to The Stationery Office Limited, St Crispins, Duke Street, Norwich NR3 1PD.

The information contained in this publication is believed to be correct at the time of manufacture. Whilst care has been taken to ensure that the information is accurate, the publisher can accept no responsibility for any errors or ommisions or for changes to the details given.

David Wathey and Mark O'Reilly have asserted their moral rights under the Copyright, Designs and Patents Act 1988, to be identified as the authors of this work.

A CIP catalogue record for this book is available from the British Library
A Library of Congress CIP catalogue record has been applied for

First published 2000

ISBN 0 11 702472 4

Printed in the United Kingdom by Albert Gait Ltd, Grimsby, N.E. Lincolnshire
TJ2529 c20 12/00 9835 13462

Contents

Acknowledgements

The authors would like to extend their gratitude to all those individuals and organisations involved in the development of this book. In particular we would like to thank Michael Jones of the DTI's Environment Directorate and Bernie Walsh of the DETR for their continued support of our work. Without your help none of this would have happened. Matthias Gelber, Etienne Yves Brutuille and Sankaran Vaideeswaran for their extensive and superb technical input and contributions, Ruth Hilary and Andy Hughes for their diligent reading and comment, Jane Elliot for her faith in the subject, Mark Barthel at BSI, and all of the participants in the DTI feasibility study, especially Gail Jones and Barbara Morton, whose work was invaluable.

For Mum and Beth,

MOR.

To Cecilia,

DW.

List of figures

List of appendices

List of abbreviations

BiE	Business in the Environment
CER	Corporate environmental report
DETR	Department for the Environement, Transport and the Regions
DTI	Department of Trade and Industry
EA	Environment Agency
EB	Environmental burden
ECI	Environmental condition indicator
EIA	Environmental impact assessment
EMAS	Eco Management and Audit Scheme
EMS	Environmental management system
ENDS	Environmental Data Services
EPE	Environmental performance evaluation
EPI	Environmental performance indicator
FSC	Forest Stewardship Council
GWP	Global warming potential
INEM	International Network of Environmental Management
ISO	International Organisation for Standardisation
ISO/TR	ISO Technical Report
LCA	Life cycle analysis
MPI	Management performance indicator
OPI	Operational performance indicator
PDCA	Plan-Do-Check-Act
PF	Potency factor
QMS	Quality management system
SC1 and 4	ISO Subcommittee 1 and 4
SEPA	Scottish Environment Protection Agency
TC207	ISO Technical Committee 207
UNEP	United Nations Environmental Programme

UU	United Utilities
VOC	Volatile organic compound
WWF	World Wide Fund for Nature

About the authors

14000 & ONE Solutions is a UK based environmental management consultancy which specialises in the application of environmental management systems (ISO14001 and EMAS) and environmental performance evaluation (EPE) techniques. The company also advises on other areas of organisational environmental management and policy and has delivered services to clients in over 20 countries world-wide. The company provides representation at ISO TC 207, SC1 and SC4, the committees responsible for the development of important standards in the ISO14000 series of standards. Furthermore the company acts as adviser to the International Network of Environmental Management (INEM) and a number of United Nations initiatives on environmental management and cleaner production.

David Wathey is a consultant with 14000 & ONE Solutions Ltd. He is currently working on projects in environmental performance evaluation, environmental management system implementation and supply chain management.

Mark O'Reilly is Commercial Director of 14000 & ONE Solutions and was project manager for the UK Department of Trade and Industry (DTI) environmental performance evaluation (EPE) project. He is currently co-ordinator of Project Acorn, the second phase of UK activity that brings together EMS and EPE in a formal programme for the first time.

Background

This book has been written to provide interpretation of the ISO14031 standard on environmental performance evaluation (EPE)[1], along with guidance and methodology for application and implementation. The book draws on practical experience gained by the authors during a UK government sponsored ISO14031 demonstration project[2].

ISO14031 forms part of the ISO14000 series, of which ISO14001 (the international standard for environmental management systems) is probably the best known; but, unlike ISO14001, ISO14031 is not a certifiable specification standard.

---

[1] The first edition of ISO14031 was published on 15 November 1999.
[2] The demonstration project was sponsored by the Department of Trade and Industry and looked at the application of the ISO14031 approach in twelve companies from different sectors and of varying scale and influence (14000 & ONE Solutions, 2000).

Chapter 1 **Introduction**

The adage, 'if you don't measure it you can't manage it', is fast becoming a catch phrase within environmental management circles. This prompts the question however, how do you measure environmental performance?

ISO14031, the international standard for environmental performance evaluation (EPE), aims to provide some answers to this question, and to offer practical guidance to organisations in selecting relevant, reliable and comparable measures of environmental performance. All too often the focus of environmental management activity has been on systems design development, which, though relevant, has often led to the principal purpose of the activity, the improvement of environmental performance and reduction of the impact on the environment, being overlooked.

Early applications of EPE principles have demonstrated that environmental management can be a value adding activity for the organisation, not merely a reactive paper chase to satisfy legislators, and the demands of customers, activists and other interested parties. Potential benefits include:

- Assistance in identifying environmental problems and benefits
- Support for decision making
- Provision of information for the tracking of performance against stated aims, objectives and targets
- Provision of tangible information to aid communication and reporting
- Facilitation of environmental benchmarking activity or assessment (internally or externally)
- Support for product environmental claims
- Helping organisations raise the profile of their environmental activity, in a credible manner
- Maintaining a clear focus for activity and providing the driver for continual environmental improvement.

This book aims to provide a practical interpretation of the ISO14031 standard, along with further guidance and methodologies, for anyone responsible for the management of environmental issues within an organisation. The book is designed to lead the user through the stages of implementing a fully functional ISO14031-based EPE system.

Despite the provision of methodologies and templates throughout the book, it is important to remember that ISO14031 is only a guidance standard, and sets no absolute conditions for application. As such, the emphasis needs to be placed on developing a flexible EPE system suitable for the scale and nature of your organisation.

1.1 Structure of the book

Background information is provided in Chapter 2, along with guidance on the first steps to implementing EPE. Chapters 3 to 5 then follow through the 'plan, do, check and act' cycle (PDCA cycle), which forms the basis of the EPE framework proposed under ISO14031. And, finally, Chapter 6 takes a brief look at various specific applications of the ISO14031 EPE approach which take it beyond merely a support tool for ISO14001 into applications such as supply chain management, environmental accounting and eco-labelling, to name but a few.

Throughout the book a range of tables, diagrams, examples and real-life case studies are used to explain points and provide insight into various approaches. In addition to this the book provides, within the appendices, a range of suggested templates, to assist the user at different stages. These templates can be used as shown, adapted to suit the needs of the user, or used merely as a point of reference.

As this book is intended as a guidebook for the implementation of an ISO14031 EPE system, a large part of it is devoted to the planning, development and implementation stages. Ongoing operation of an ISO14031 EPE system is touched upon, as this will require attention, but the nature of the activity involved will very much be shaped by the nature of the system and the organisation within which it operates.

Figure 1 outlines the principal stages of the ISO14031 planning, development, implementation and operation process, as outlined in this book. The different shading of the boxes in this diagram indicates how each stage relates to chapters of the book.

Figure 1 ISO14031 EPE system implementation process map

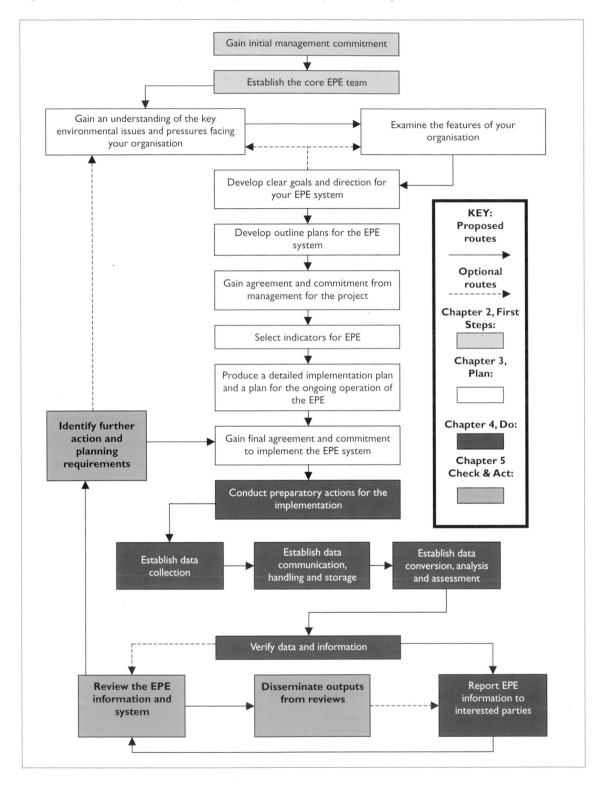

At the start of each main section within Chapters 2 to 5, a task template provides a brief summary of the key elements of the stage, detailing:

* The task heading
* Section reference
* An indication of duration and difficulty
* Aims and objectives of the stage
* Anticipated outputs from the stage
* Considerations for resources required in the section (in terms of people and physical resources)
* Required outputs from previous tasks
* Potential problems and opportunities.

The task template is only intended as a summary overview, so that the user can quickly assess the implications of the stage; it should not be relied upon solely, and different organisational scenarios may render some of the information irrelevant.

The duration and difficulty-rating boxes on the task template are provided as a rough guide to assist you in planning, and in assessing the work involved at each stage. The duration is based upon an estimate of the minimum time required within a simple, small, single-location organisation. The difficulty rating is based on a 1 to 5 scale with 1 being the least difficult, through to 5, the most difficult. Again, this is based on general experience and will vary from organisation to organisation, but it is hoped that it will provide some insight into the nature of the activity required at each stage.

Similarly, resource considerations, and potential problems and opportunities, are only a suggested list based upon experience, and it is likely that many users will find other entries which apply more specifically to them.

1.2 How to use the book

The book presents the ISO14031 EPE process in linear fashion in order to provide some clarity and structure. However, projects are very rarely this straightforward, and depending on the circumstances of the organisation and user, the approach taken will probably deviate from this linear route to a greater or lesser extent.

The step-by-step presentation is aimed at helping the user to structure the approach to EPE implementation, but the system eventually developed and implemented needs to serve the purposes of the organisation; it is not intended that the book become a prescriptive strait-jacket.

We trust that this book will prove to be a useful companion on the route to evaluating environmental performance and to meeting the ever-increasing environmental aspirations of parties within and without the organisation.

Chapter 2 *Establishing the Foundation*

At the end of this chapter you should have a basic understanding of what environmental performance evaluation (EPE) is, and how it relates to ISO14031 and other environmental management tools and standards. In addition to this you should have gained an understanding of the framework of, and principles applied to, EPE development and operation under the ISO14031 approach. By following each stage in this section you will have developed an initial vision of what you want to achieve, and put in place the foundations for building an EPE system within your organisation.

The principal outputs of this chapter will be:

* An understanding of what EPE and ISO14031 are
* An understanding of the principles of EPE and ISO14031
* A vision of what you want the EPE system to achieve for the organisation
* An outline plan, with timescales and milestones, for developing an EPE system
* An outline of resource requirements to achieve initial milestones
* The securing of initial top management commitment
* Identification of a project manager
* Establishment of a 'core EPE team'.

Task Heading	**What are EPE and ISO14031?**
Section Reference	**2.1**
Duration	0.5 man days +
Difficulty Rating	1
Aims & Objectives	By reading through this section you should develop a basic understanding of what EPE is, and how it relates to ISO14031 and other environmental management tools and standards.
Outputs	At the end of this section you should understand: • What EPE is • What ISO14031 is, and what it is not • What ISO14032 is • The linkages between ISO14031 and ISO14001 • The scope and suitability of ISO14031 EPE • The objective of the ISO14031 approach to EPE • The role of ISO14031 EPE as an environmental management tool • The relationship between ISO14031 EPE and other environmental management tools and standards • The applications and benefits of ISO14031 EPE • The critical factors for a successful ISO14031 EPE.

Resources Considerations
    People
    Physical
	Project initiator
	Access to information

Outputs from Previous Tasks	Understanding of the purpose, structure and format of this guidebook, and how it is intended to be used. Sections 1.1, 1.2
Potential Problems	• Limited experience of environmental management • Low levels of environmental awareness and understanding.
Potential Opportunities	• Develop a clear understanding of what EPE and ISO14031 are • Build environmental awareness • Identify significant benefits which EPE could bring to your organisation.

2.1.1 What is EPE?

Environmental performance evaluation (EPE) is a collective term for the measurement and analysis of factors which are recognised as having a direct or indirect impact on the environment.

An EPE system is the collection of procedures and practices which are put in place to facilitate the evaluation of environmental performance. Guidance, training, resources allocation and support are likely to be required as well to enable any EPE system to function, and therefore the detail of these features is often assumed to be within the system.

At an organisational level, EPE is a management-driven process which can provide information on past and present performance, and indicate possible future performance. The information provided can be used to track environmental performance over time, or at any point, against environmental criteria established by the organisation or external interested parties. EPE, applied in this context, can provide valuable information to management, when identifying problems and successes, making informed decisions and implementing action to remedy or enhance performance.

EPE focuses on the use of tangible measures, as opposed to attempting qualitative evaluation of performance, working very much on the principle, that 'what gets measured, gets managed' or perhaps more accurately 'if you don't measure it, you can't manage it'.

2.1.2 What is ISO14031?

ISO14031 is the international standard for environmental performance evaluation, and forms part of the ISO14000 series, of which ISO14001, the international standard for environmental management systems (EMSs), is probably the best known. ISO14031 is a guidance standard only, unlike ISO14001, which is a specification standard. This means that you cannot be certified to ISO14031.

ISO14031 is intended to provide guidance for the establishment and operation of EPE within an organisation, and establishes some standard terminology and a framework for the development of an EPE system. The reporting suggested within the standard is aimed purely at facilitating the internal communication and management of environmental performance. Subsequent approaches to EPE have looked at wider applications, and have adopted ISO14031 to provide a standardised approach. These wider applications include external corporate environmental reporting, the management of environmental performance in supply chains, support for product eco-labelling, environmental accounting and various benchmarking exercises looking at environmental performance and risk.

ISO14031 does not establish any specific indicators or measures which organisations should adopt, and does not stipulate any absolute performance criteria which should be met. Furthermore, ISO14031 does not dictate the methods used for data collection, analysis or reporting. These decisions are left up to the organisation, which should establish methods, measures and criteria that are suitable to its size, scale and nature, and address its key environmental issues, pressures, aspects and impacts.

2.1.3 What is ISO14032?

ISO14032 is an ISO technical report developed to support the ISO14031 guidance standard. The purpose of the report is to provide practical case-study examples of EPE application to assist organisations in improving their understanding of the guidance in ISO14031 and its application.

2.1.4 The scope and suitability of ISO14031 EPE

The ISO14031 standard has been designed to be applicable to all organisations. Although originally envisaged as guidance to be used in conjunction with the environmental management systems standard ISO14001, it has subsequently been recognised for its potential in facilitating the introduction of ISO14001, or as a stand-alone environmental management tool.

2.1.5 The objective of the ISO14031 approach to EPE

The objective of the ISO14031 approach to EPE is to provide an environmental management tool which helps organisations establish their level of environmental performance. From this, organisations can clearly identify and establish programmes for improving environmental performance based upon thorough assessment of tangible information.

2.1.6 The linkages between ISO14031 and ISO14001

As already mentioned, ISO14031 and ISO14001 are both standards within the ISO14000 series. ISO14031 was developed to complement ISO14001, especially in the more quantifiable elements, and uses many of the standard terms found in ISO14001.

Having said this, ISO14031 does differ from ISO14001 in certain areas, most strikingly in the definition of environmental performance (see section 2.2.1).

2.1.7 The relationship between ISO14031 and other environmental management tools and standards

As with the relationship with ISO14001, ISO14031 also overlaps with some other commonly applied environmental management tools and standards, especially where these tools and standards require quantifiable information on the environmental activities of the organisation.

The facilitation of environmental reporting within the organisation is a stated aim of ISO14031, but this can equally be extended to external reporting should the organisation so wish. Indeed, recent trends have seen a dramatic increase in the external reporting of environmental information by organisations, and this looks set to continue. EMAS (Eco Management and Audit Scheme) makes external reporting a requirement; ISO14031 could assist companies in meeting this.

Environmental project, and product, evaluation and planning tools often rely on large amounts of quantified environmental information, which is commonly estimated or assumed. ISO14031 EPE has the potential to provide more-reliable actual data for such tools and processes, if designed with this application in mind. Examples of tools which might benefit from ISO14031 EPE information include environmental impact assessment (EIA), the 'natural step', and life-cycle analysis (LCA).

The use of financial terminology in project evaluation is common where cost-benefit analysis or return-on-investment predictions are required. ISO14031 EPE can be developed to address costs and benefits, and state these in financial terms. This will also be useful in environmental accounting activities which go further than project evaluation to track costs and benefits accruing through the organisation's operations.

2.1.8 The role of ISO14031 EPE as an environmental management tool

In addition to providing information on environmental performance to assist management in identifying and establishing environmental programmes, an ISO14031 EPE system can provide continual information on the implementation and operation of programmes. This will allow for assessment of progress against established targets, forecasts or performance criteria, and the benchmarking of comparable elements of the organisation and/or external groups.

Improving knowledge of practices and performances, past and present, allows for predictions and forecasts to be based on more-reliable information, which in turn will assist planning, and allow organisations to manage the expectations of interested parties more effectively. In respect of this last point, ISO14031 can provide an effective vehicle for the application of environmental performance monitoring initiatives at an international, national, local or sector level.

Further to this, ISO14031 can be a useful tool for providing:

- Information to support reporting and communications through the organisation, and to external parties (should it so choose).
- Information on a product's environmental characteristics and/or performance.
- An indication of environmental risk exposure.
- Information to support environmental accounting practices and procedures.
- Information on the environmental probity of key interested parties within the supply chain.

These applications of ISO14031 are discussed in Chapter 6 of this book.

2.1.9 Benefits of ISO14031 EPE

An ISO14031 EPE system, as we have seen, will provide information on the environmental performance of the organisation. This information can be used to derive a number of benefits for the organisation. It:

- Supports analysis, evaluation and decision-making processes
- Enables important issues, pressures, aspects and impacts to be identified, and in turn the development of a meaningful focus for environmental activity
- Supports the tracking of performance against key factors, and allows more-accurate prediction of likely outcomes, enabling the organisation to become proactive, as opposed to reacting to external pressures and legislative requirements
- Supports the reporting of environmental information to key interested parties which can be substantiated and in terms which are meaningful to those parties
- Enables organisations to gain competitive advantage by being able to provide customers and consumers with information on issues of concern to them
- Can help organisations raise the profile of their environmental activity in a credible manner
- Can be used effectively to motivate staff and management in relation to environmental activity and performance
- Allows for the comparison of environmental performance between parties internally and externally
- Allows for the evaluation of environmental performance in terms of management effort, as well as environmental impact, or the condition of the environment
- Can demonstrate the value added for the organisation through environmental activity (in financial or non-financial terms).

In relation to an ISO14001 EMS, ISO14031 offers particular benefits by:

- Helping to focus activity on achieving objectives and targets established
- Providing the means by which an organisation can monitor and demonstrate continual improvement
- Providing reliable information for the assessment of significant aspects and impacts
- Providing reliable information in a quantitative format to support internal communications
- Providing quantitative information on the EMS development and operation in key areas or clauses.

2.1.10 The critical factors for a successful ISO14031 EPE system

Four key features lie at the heart of a successful ISO14031 EPE system:

- An understanding of the issues and their relative importance
- Clearly defined and achievable direction and goals which complement existing aims and aspirations of the organisation
- Commitment from top management
- Efficient and effective communications.

Once you have these in place you will need to consider more-practical issues, such as resource and time implications. The extent of resources and time required for a successful ISO14031 EPE will vary with the organisation and with the approach adopted. Whatever the circumstances, resource requirements and timescales will need to be clearly identified and provided for throughout the implementation and operation of the EPE system.

In addition to resources, you will have to be mindful of the skills and competencies which are available to the organisation, and ensure that these are sufficient to support your planned activity. Awareness raising, training and support are likely to be required across a range of activities and functions within the organisation. The involvement of parties across the organisation will be required, and thus commitment will need to be gained not only at the level of top management but at other levels as well.

Efficient and effective data collection, communication, analysis, verification and review processes will be required in operation of the EPE system, if it is to be a success. Ultimately the ISO14031 EPE should be able to demonstrate tangible benefit for the organisation and its users.

Task Heading	**Principles of the ISO14031 EPE approach**
Section Reference	**2.2**
Duration	0.5 man days +
Difficulty Rating	1
Aims & Objectives	By reading through this section you should have gained an understanding of the framework and principles applied to EPE development and operation under the ISO14031 approach.
Outputs	At the end of this section you should understand: • What environmental performance is • The role of indicators • The five characteristics of indicator expression • The categories of indicators • The distinction between environmental performance and environmental condition • The principle of the PDCA cycle.
Resources Considerations *People* *Physical*	Project initiator Access to information
Outputs from Previous Tasks	An understanding of EPE and how it relates to ISO14031 and other environmental management tools and standards. Section 2.1
Potential Problems	• Limited experience of environmental management • Low levels of environmental awareness and understanding.
Potential Opportunities	• Develop a clear understanding of the framework and principles of the ISO14031 approach to EPE • Build environmental awareness • Identify significant benefits which EPE could bring to your organisation.

2.2.1 What is environmental performance?

The definition of environmental performance tends to differ from publication to publication. Indeed the definition given in ISO14031 differs from that given in ISO14001. Figure 2 gives both of these for your reference.

Figure 2 Definitions of environmental performance

	Environmental performance is:
ISO14031 (1999)	'the results of an organisation's management of its environmental aspects'
ISO14001 (1996)	'the measurable results of the environmental management system, related to an organisation's control of its environmental aspects, based on its environmental policy, objectives and targets'

Environmental performance can be expressed in many different ways. For example:
- Change in the physical impact on the environment
- The rate of change of impact on the environment
- The financial evaluation of the impact on the environment
- The level of achievement of environmental objectives, targets or criteria established by the organisation
- Change in the impact on the environment in relation to the organisation's activity.

It may well be necessary to express environmental performance in a number of different ways according to whom you are communicating with, for different interested parties will have different concerns, requirements and levels of understanding.

Care needs to be taken to ensure that performance is expressed using terminology that is meaningful to the intended recipients.

2.2.2 The role of indicators in ISO14031

Indicators (commonly referred to as metrics[1]) are central to the structure of an ISO14031 EPE system, providing information about different aspects of environmental performance and management at various levels within an organisation. Note that it is possible however that indicators can be applied beyond the conventional bounds of the organisation as well, in such cases as the assessment of suppliers' environmental performance, customer environmental risk or the condition of the environment in general.

---

[1] The differentiation between indicators and metrics made by some texts is not particularly helpful and does not feature in ISO14031. This book will adopt the ISO14031 approach and refer to indicators at all stages.

ISO14031 suggests the use of a range of indicators to track performance against key environmental issues or goals, and this in turn will support management decision-making processes.

An indicator defines a set (or sets) of information and the terms in which it is (or they are) expressed.

Example 1: an indicator could be the total tonnes of waste sent to land fill. In which case the data set would be the tonnage of all waste sent to land fill, expressed as an absolute figure.

Example 2: Alternatively, an indicator could be the amount of waste sent to land fill as a percentage of all waste generated. In this case the indicator specifies two data sets, the tonnage of all waste sent to land fill, and the tonnage of all waste generated (regardless of disposal route), expressing landfill waste as a percentage of total waste.

2.2.3 Five characteristics of indicator expression

ISO14031 establishes standard terminology to characterise the five principal methods by which an indicator can be expressed.

- Direct: basic data which have not been changed in any way (as per Example 1).
- Relative: data compared to or relative to another set of data (as per Example 2).
- Indexed: data are converted into units which relate to a standard or baseline. For example, if total waste sent to land fill in year one was 50,000 tonnes and this was set as the baseline year with an index of 100, year two tonnage sent to land fill, being 53,000 tonnes, would have an index value of 106.
- Aggregated: data in the same terms are combined to give an overall figure. For example, total tonnes of waste sent to land fill for all company operating sites. In some cases it is possible to convert data using different terms into standard terms. However, care needs to be taken to ensure that the conversion methodology applied is reliable and suitable, or at least that any limitations are understood.
- Weighted: data are modified by applying a factor that aims to represent the relative significance of the data set. For example, methane has been shown to contribute to global warming nineteen times more per unit volume than CO_2. In this instance, a company emitting both methane and CO_2, may choose to multiply methane volumes by nineteen (to arrive at a CO_2 equivalent measure) before comparing them with CO_2 emission volumes (see Figure 3). Scientifically proven significance relationships are not common however, and it is important to take care if applying weighting factors to data, to ensure that results are reliable and not overly influenced by subjectivity.

Figure 3   **Example of weighting**

Dig & Dump Waste Management Company			
Gas Emitted	Tonnes	Global Warming Potential	CO_2 Tonnes Equivalent
Methane	30,000	19	570,000
CO_2	4,000	1	4,000
Total Emissions	**34,000**	**N/A**	**574,000**

Direct and relative terms of expression are easier to collate and generally more widely understood, with the units of measurement generally being more meaningful to interested parties.

Indexed indicators allow for data to be simplified into more-manageable terms and can offer consistent terminology even under circumstances of great change. For example, an organisation which is changing the number of sites year on year can adjust the base figures accordingly but still report meaningfully on an indicator in index terms.

Aggregation and weighting allow for greater comparison of data sets, but will often require a greater understanding from the users and recipients if they are to be effective management tools.

As you develop the EPE system, so the relative merits of each category of expression will become apparent. This does not suggest, however, that all categories of expression will be right for use in all EPE systems, as this will be driven very much by the nature of the data involved and the parties to whom the information is to be communicated and/or by whom it is to be used.

2.2.4   Categories of indicators

In addition to identifying characteristics for terms of expression, ISO14031 also identifies categories of indicators based on the sort of data sets which it specifies. Figure 4 outlines the categories of indicators referred to in ISO14031.

Figure 4 **ISO14031 Categories of indicators**

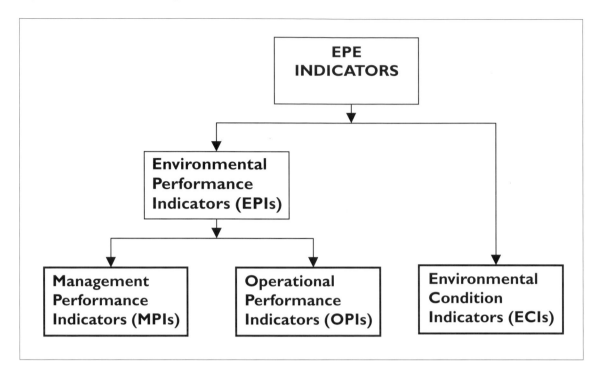

An environmental condition indicator (ECI) is defined as 'providing information about the local, regional, national or global condition of the environment' (ISO14031, 1999).

Examples of ECIs:
local: average water temperature adjacent to company discharge point;
regional: number of corn buntings observed in the region at last district bird population census;
national: national average blood lead levels in humans;
global: hectares of tropical rainforest cleared in last year.

As can be seen from the examples given, the level of influence an organisation is likely to be able to exert on an ECI diminishes the less localised the ECI. Given this, organisations tend to prefer selecting local ECIs which they can exert some control over (albeit not exclusively).

An environmental performance indicator (EPI) is defined as 'providing information about an organisation's environmental performance' (ISO14031, 1999), and can be either an MPI or an OPI.

A management performance indicator (MPI) is defined as 'providing information about the management efforts to influence the organisation's environmental performance' (ISO14031, 1999).

Examples of MPIs:

number of prevention-of-pollution initiatives implemented;

percentage of employees to receive refresher training to schedule;

index of costs resulting from environmental incidents (referenced to 1990 baseline);

monetary investment in environmental projects in last financial period;

weighted score for environmental complaints received in last month.

An operational performance indicator (OPI) is defined as 'providing information about the environmental performance of an organisation's operations' (ISO14031, 1999).

OPIs focus on the activities, products and services of an organisation and in some circumstances may be extended to cover the supply chain as well. The key areas for consideration when establishing OPIs are illustrated in Figure 5.

Figure 5   Key areas to consider in establishing OPIs

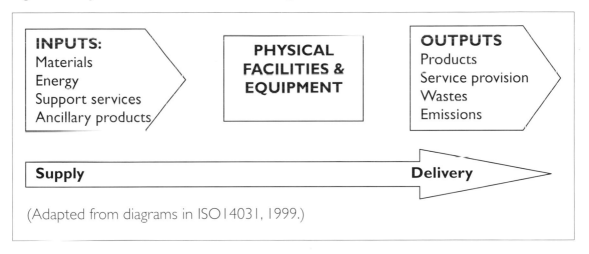

INPUTS:
Materials
Energy
Support services
Ancillary products

PHYSICAL FACILITIES & EQUIPMENT

OUTPUTS
Products
Service provision
Wastes
Emissions

Supply   Delivery

(Adapted from diagrams in ISO14031, 1999.)

Examples of OPIs:

tonnes of raw material used per 100,000 units of production;

KW hours of electricity consumed per hour of operation;

volume of hazardous material used by contract cleaners;

average water consumption per employee;

average distance travelled per service call out;

percentage of product packaging that can be recycled;

number of warranty call outs within one year of purchase or renewal.

2.2.5   Environmental performance or environmental condition?

The distinction between environmental performance indicators (MPIs and OPIs) and environmental condition indicators (ECIs) is made because the organisation has direct influence over MPIs and OPIs and thus can make efforts to improve its environmental performance under such indicators. ECIs, on the other hand, relate to the condition of the natural environment, or a specific element thereof, which although potentially affected by the activities, products or services of the organisation can also be affected by many other factors or parties over which the organisation does not necessarily exert any control or influence.

Figure 6 highlights the relationship between the different classifications of indicator within ISO14031.

Figure 6 **The relationship between the different classifications of indicator**

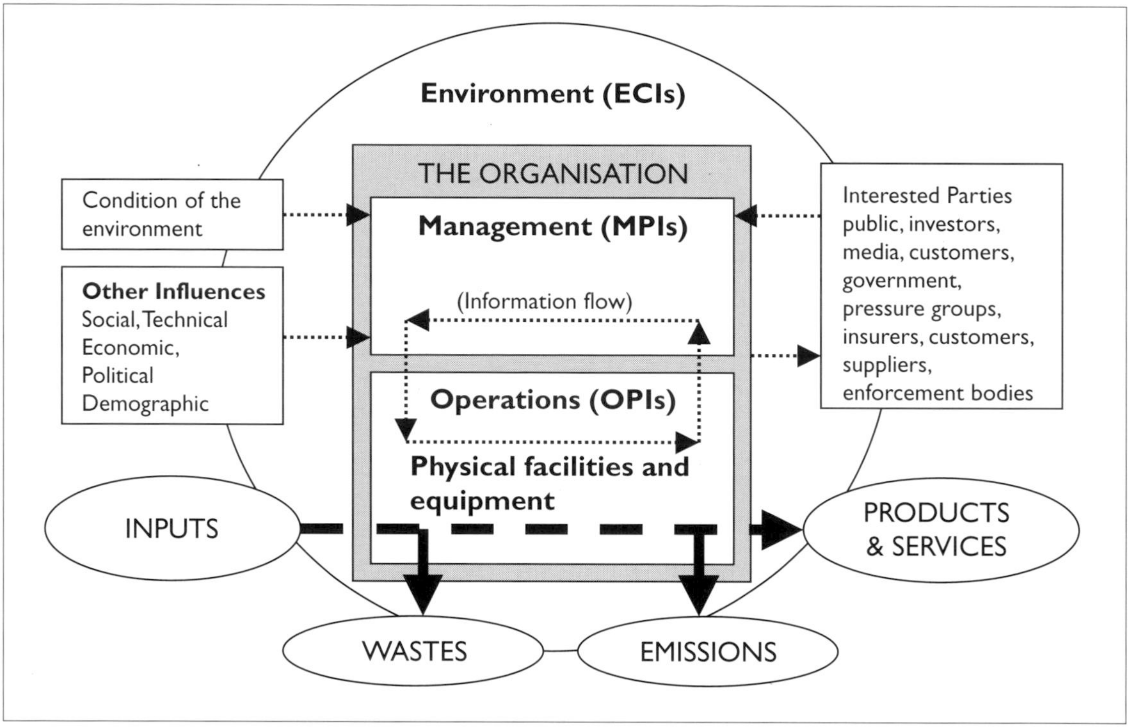

(Adapted from Figure 2, p.5, ISO14031, 1999,)

2.2.6 How does ISO14031 work? The PDCA cycle

The basis of the ISO14031 approach to EPE is the 'Plan, Do, Check and Act' model or PDCA model. This is sometimes referred to as the Deming model. It has been used as the basis for a number of management standards, including ISO9000 and ISO14001, and follows a simple, continuous process, as illustrated in Figure 7.

Figure 7 **The PDCA model**

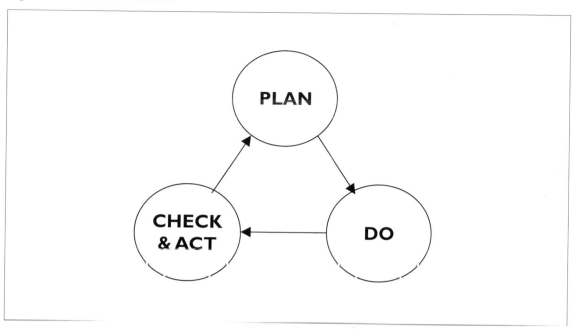

We will take a detailed look at what each of these phases entails under ISO14031 in the following sections, but Figure 8 below outlines for your reference the principal requirements of each phase.

As the PDCA model follows a continuous cycle, you should find that the requirements under 'check and act' begin to feed into the 'plan' and 'do' phases of the next cycle.

Figure 8   **Required actions for EPE under ISO14031**

PHASE	REQUIRED ACTIONS

PLAN	• To understand the key issues and their relative importance, assess:
	  ○ significant environmental aspects and impacts
	  ○ any environmental performance criteria
	  ○ views of interested parties
	  ○ legal requirements
	  ○ environmental costs and benefits
	
	• To understand features of your organisation, assess:
	  ○ existing practices and procedures
	  ○ organisational structure
	  ○ organisational culture
	  ○ potential barriers and opportunities
	• Define clear direction and goals
	• Secure top management commitment
	• Select indicators for environmental performance evaluation
	• Produce an implementation plan
	• Produce an operational plan
	• Gain final approval and commitment.

DO	• Implementation of plans • Establish data collection processes and systems • Establish data communication processes and systems • Devise data conversion, analysis and assessment processes and systems • Provide for verification of data and information outputs • Establish processes and systems for reporting, presenting and communicating information to relevant interested parties.
CHECK & ACT	• Implement the review structure, schedule and format • Review environmental performance information • Review feedback from interested parties • Review goals and targets, and amend if necessary • Seek continually to improve the EPE system • Develop action plans to improve or correct environmental performance (PLAN).

Task Heading	**First steps**
Section Reference	**2.3**
Duration	9 man days +
Difficulty Rating	2
Aims & Objectives	By following each step in this section you will have developed an initial vision of what you want to achieve, and put in place the foundations for building an EPE system within your organisation.
Outputs	The principal outputs of this section will be: • A vision of what you want the EPE system to achieve for the organisation • An outline plan, with timescales and milestones, for developing an EPE system • An outline of resource requirements to achieve initial milestones • The securing of initial top management commitment • Establishment of a project manager • Establishment of a 'core EPE team'.
Resources Considerations People	Project initiator Top management Advisers and consultants
Physical	Work station and office facilities Access to information Commercial tools and packages (based on software or hard copy) Meetings facilities Access to presentation materials, equipment and media
Outputs from Previous Tasks	An understanding of EPE and how it relates to ISO14031 and other environmental management tools and standards. Section 2.1 An understanding of the framework and principles applied to EPE development and operation under the ISO14031 approach. Section 2.2
Potential Problems	• Lack of top management commitment • Little or no pressure to improve environmental performance • Lack of resources • Limited experience of environmental management • Limited project management experience • Low levels of environmental awareness and understanding.
Potential Opportunities	• Realisation of benefits (see section 2.1.9) • Enhancing the credibility of environmental management activity with key interested parties • Building relationships with top management • The provision of tangible and credible information to assist management in various functions and tasks.

2.3.1　What do you want to achieve?

The principal outputs of this stage will be:

○　A brainstorming list of the key environmental issues and pressures facing your organisation

○　Additions to the brainstorming list of any environmental aspirations of your organisation

○　Identification of the areas of the brainstorming list where an ISO14031 EPE system can bring benefits

○　The summary of this information to support future communications or presentations

○　The initial vision of what you want to achieve with the application of ISO14031 and implementation of EPE

2.3.1.1　Brainstorming key environmental issues and pressures

In order to understand which of the potential benefits offered by the ISO14031 approach to EPE will be applicable, or of real value, to your organisation, you must first have some idea of the key environmental issues and pressures facing it. As touched upon in section 2.2, these issues and pressures can come from many different sources.

Appendix 1 provides a template to use for the brainstorming of key environmental issues and pressures facing your organisation. Some common examples are given to prompt this process but these may not all apply, and other pressures or issues may exist which are not mentioned. For this reason, you can delete those issues and pressures which do not apply, and add in any not listed.

The brainstorming process might also be facilitated by considering the following common sources of environmental issues and pressures:

- Global environmental issues
- Political responses to environmental issues
- Social reaction to the environment
- Technical advances and scientific discovery
- Economic influences
- Legal liability
- Financial risks
- Moral accountability
- Financial performance
- Market forces

- Views of interested parties
- Corporate values and aspirations

2.3.1.2 Brainstorming the environmental aspirations of your organisation

In addition to the environmental issues and pressures facing your organisation, it is possible that top management, and other interested parties, may well have aspirations for environmental management activity and performance that go beyond merely addressing internal drivers. Make sure you give some thought to this. It might be worth discussing environmental issues and aspirations with key people within the organisation to gauge opinions and fundamental values.

Any aspirations for improving environmental management and/or performance should be added to the list of issues and pressures developed in section 2.3.1.1. The template in Appendix 1 provides a few common organisational aspirations as examples and prompts.

2.3.1.3 Identifying the benefits of ISO14031

The brainstorming process described in sections 2.3.1.1 and 2.3.1.2 should have produced a list of environmental issues, pressures and aspirations (these will be referred to as 'drivers' from now onwards). The aim of this stage is to highlight where ISO14031 can add the most value to your organisation, by addressing the principal environmental drivers.

The template in Appendix 1 provides space to note, against each environmental driver, how ISO14031 can help the organisation address it in a way that will benefit the organisation. Some examples have been identified on the template to help you, and section 2.1.8 might also provide useful reference on some of the potential benefits of applying ISO14031 EPE in an organisation.

Space is also provided on the template to rate the value-adding potential (or importance) for each driver and/or benefit. This approach may well help you in summarising and prioritising the drivers and benefits identified.

2.3.1.4 Summarising drivers and benefits

Depending on how you have conducted the brainstorming process, you might find it useful to summarise the outputs for future reference or as supporting evidence.

Prioritising the drivers and benefits identified can help to focus further actions, and strengthen the message when presenting to secure commitment.

The summarisation of the information in a logical, clear and presentable manner may save time in the future when reviewing or communicating the information.

2.3.1.5 Developing the vision

The aim of this step is to develop a clear and concise 'vision' of what you want to achieve through the development of an ISO14031 EPE system. This vision need not be documented or widely communicated, and indeed it will probably evolve over the course of the process. However, developing this initial vision will help focus any further efforts, and also support any dissemination and commitment-gaining activity.

A simple example of an initial vision statement is given below, though the style, content and presentation needs to be decided by you.

Example vision statement

The development of an ISO14031 EPE system for ABC Inc. will facilitate the maintenance of the environmental management system and the delivery of continual improvement. The system will provide information to help manage:

- The reduction of risk of pollution incidents

- The continued compliance with relevant legislation

- The minimisation of material consumption and waste generation

- The reduction of harmful emissions to atmosphere

- The regular reporting of environmental management activity to shareholders and employees.

2.3.2 Outline planning for ISO14031

The principal outputs from this stage will be:

O   The identification of the tasks to be completed

O   The identification of timescales for the completion of the tasks

O   The identification of milestones for gauging achievements

O   An outline task and timescale plan which encapsulates the information identified in the steps above, and possibly a summary thereof.

Identifying tasks to be completed

The aim of this step is to identify the tasks to be completed for the implementation of an ISO14031 EPE system. You may find that if you have implemented an environmental management system (e.g. ISO14001) you will have already completed some of these tasks.

Unless you have some form of EPE system in place already, it is likely that most attention will need to be paid to tasks under the planning phase, and probably only the first stages of this phase.

Figure 8 (p.35), and the task templates at the beginning of each main section of Chapters 3 to 5, identify the principal tasks required, and you may choose to use these as reference to help you identify and structure the activities. Appendix 2 provides a template to assist you with the preparation of the outline plan. This has some key tasks already entered for you, but also provides space for you to add further tasks if required.

Remember, this outline plan is intended to support you in securing initial top management commitment, and you will need some feel for overall project timescales and costs as well as some detail on what needs doing next.

Identifying timescales for the completion of tasks

Using the template from Appendix 2 with the tasks to be completed identified on it, you can now embark on attaching timescales to the completion of those tasks. The template provides a grid for you to apply your own time units (e.g. days, weeks, months, periods, etc.).

In defining the timescales required to complete each task, it is likely that you will need to take account of resources and skills availability. This will be covered in the next section (2.3.3), so it might prove useful to consider sections 2.3.2 and 2.3.3 together. And note again, the existence of a formal EMS may well reduce the timescales for completing certain tasks.

This process will help you identify what time you have available to complete tasks, and what level of resources you will require to meet those timescales.

Whatever the circumstances, it will be necessary to have a projected completion date for the project, to give credibility to the process, and support you in securing top management commitment.

Identifying exact timescales required to complete tasks will be difficult at this early stage for all but the most immediate tasks. It must be noted that the duration indications given for each main section and stage are minimum guidelines based on a very simple and small-scale organisation. In addition, note that they work on man days, not actual calendar duration. However, they might prove useful as an indication of relative time requirements.

The main point at this stage is to be realistic in your predictions. Some tips are provided below for consideration.

- Allow for some slippage in the time schedule, especially when planning over long timeframes. This will accommodate unforeseen events and problems
- Build in realistic time when input, review or feedback is required from other parties.
- Senior management, external parties and geographically dispersed parties will often be less accessible or available.
- Communications media will have an influence on timescales, particularly at the detailed level.
- Groups can reduce timescales if tasks can be spread between members, but can increase timescales if not.
- Allow for holidays, peak business periods, seasonally affected tasks and restrictions imposed by financial periods.
- Allow time for skills and knowledge building, and gaining experience.
- Ensure that interdependent tasks are scheduled in sequence.

As part of the process of identifying timescales for completing tasks, it can prove valuable to note any assumptions made in the calculation of the timescale. This will help you support your initial proposals, but also help you identify areas which require further resource input, or where savings can be made, as you progress through the programme and experience is gained. Appendix 2 provides space to make notes against each task.

2.3.2.3 Identifying milestones

The aim of this step is to identify milestones and timescale targets for the outline plan. Identified milestones can be entered on the planning template in Appendix 2.

Milestones are points in the process that are seen as significant from a review and progress-monitoring perspective.

Identifying milestones once timescales have been defined provides a clear way of measuring progress towards the implementation of the EPE system.

Targets can be set for reaching these milestones. These targets will often assist communication and motivation, and help ensure that the process meets projected timescales.

Examples of such targets are:

- The completion of the planning phase - by week 12
- The securing of initial top management commitment - by June
- The selection of a core EPE team - by period end
- The identification of all aspects and impacts for production unit C - before annual shutdown
- The production of the first annual company environmental report - to coincide with the end of year financial statement
- The receipt of the first six months' data by the data analysis team - by the end of month 7.

Milestones are useful for maintaining the momentum and focus through lengthy or complex tasks, and thus some significant points in the process can seem relatively minor when compared to others.

As accurate planning at such an early stage is generally difficult, the establishment of milestones allows for flexibility in the implementation, providing that the milestones are achieved.

2.3.2.4 Summarising the outline activity and timescale plan

The need to summarise the outline plan will depend upon the approach you have taken in developing the plan, the level of detail and complexity, and how you intend to use the plan.

The template in Appendix 2 should prove sufficient for summarising the outline plan, if not presenting the whole plan. Additional supporting notes might be required to explain the rationale applied, if a high degree of summarisation has been carried out.

Well-presented activity and timescale plans can prove to be a very effective means of communicating complex and detailed plans. The use of colour and symbols in a simple and clear format can enhance the effectiveness of such plans.

Figure 9 provides an example section of an outline plan.

Figure 9 **Example section of an outline plan**

Task / Month	J	F	M	A	M	J	J	A	S	O	N	D
First steps	■											
Securing initial top management commitment		M 1										
Understanding key issues			M 2	M 3	M 4							
Features of the organisation					M 4							
Defining direction and goals												
Securing further top management commitment							M 5					
Selecting indicators												
Producing implementation plan									M 6			

■   Completed task

     Planned timescale for completing task

M   Milestone

2.3.3 **Resource requirements**

The principal outputs of this stage will be:

O   The identification of labour input into the project

O   The identification of training and skills building requirements

O   The identification of specialist input into the project

O   The identification of facilities and infrastructure (including equipment, tools and materials) required

O   The identification of ancillary and support services required

O	The identification of contingency funds
O	The identification of the cost implications for all of the above
O	A summary breakdown of predicted resource requirments and associated costs
O	A proposal presentation to facilitate securing top management commitment based on the outputs of this section
O	Arrangements for communicating or presenting the proposal to top management.

2.3.3.1 The identification of resource requirements

Given the early stage of the project, accurately forecasting resource requirements through to completion will be difficult. Therefore, in forecasting resource requirements, it will be important to note any assumptions you have made in calculating the requirements, and also to make users of the information understand that it is an initial estimate.

Appendix 3 presents a template that can be used to record identified resource requirements against each task (or group of tasks). In addition to this, the template provides space to enter any costings, and also space to make notes on assumptions. Appendix 2 (the outline planning template) provides space to enter the names of responsible individuals or groups, labour input and total resource costs.

Some considerations for each of the resource elements identified in the task template are listed below.

Labour input:

- Expressed in man hours or as a block of time (e.g. days, weeks, months, etc.).
- Identification of specific individuals (if possible).
- Identification of project managers, 'core EPE team' members, project administration and support staff, in relation to the project implementation.
- Identification of labour input required for the implementation and operation of the EPE system, as far as possible.

Training and skills building:

- Time required delivering, or attending, training, briefing and knowledge-gathering sessions should be accounted for
- Specialist training or instructional input, from internal functions or external agencies
- The hire or purchase of training and presentation facilities and media
- Travel costs associated with training and presentations.

Specialist input:

- Technical advice and support from within the company
- Use of skills and experience from within the company
- Hire of consultants or specialist advisory services (e.g. environmental legal specialists, pollution-monitoring services)
- IT and communications specialists
- Government bodies, free or assisted support schemes
- Academic research institutions.

Facilities and infrastructure:

- Monitoring and measuring equipment
- Communications infrastructure (e.g. intranet, e-mail, fax machines)
- Data handling and storage equipment and materials
- Data analysis, handling, storage and reporting software (if in electronic format)
- Project management tools, guidance information
- Project and systems management facilities (e.g. computers, work stations, filing cabinets, etc.).

Ancillary and support services:

- Administrational support
- Travel agents
- Caterers
- Calibration services
- Equipment servicing and maintenance
- IT support and data backup
- Printers and publishers
- Publicity agents and public relations departments.

Contingency provision:

- Finance to support remedial or unforeseen activity
- Spare resources to accommodate unforeseen problems.

Where possible, the resources identified against each task should be costed in order to assist in the preparation of a project budget. Working with the outline plan developed from the template in Appendix 2 this will assist in planning costs over the duration of the project.

At this stage the lack of funds, or cash-flow problems, at certain times may well require the revision of the outline task and timescale plan developed in section 2.3.2.

2.3.3.2 Summary breakdown of predicted resource requirements and associated costs

The need to summarise resource requirements and costs will depend upon the approach you have taken, the level of detail and complexity, and how you intend to use the information generated.

The template in Appendix 3 should prove sufficient for summarising the outputs. Additional supporting notes might be required to explain the rationale applied, particularly where true costs are difficult to establish.

As mentioned in section 2.3.2.4, well-presented activity and timescale plans can prove to be a very effective means of communicating complex and detailed plans. To enhance the level of information communicated on such a plan it is useful to add individuals or groups identified as responsible for tasks, and also to add cost information by task or group of tasks. Appendix 2 (the outline plan template) provides boxes for this information to be added if required.

2.3.3.3 Developing the proposal

The purpose of developing a proposal is to facilitate the securing of initial top management commitment.

The style and content of the proposal will be dependent upon the expectations of the group or individual whom you will need to convince. In view of this you will need to gear the proposal to highlight the areas of interest for your organisation's top management, and in a style which is acceptable to and easily understood by them.

Four key questions which are likely to be foremost in the minds of top management are:

- What benefits will the project deliver?
- How much will it cost?
- How long will it take?
- Why should we support this project over alternative proposals?

You should make the answers to these questions stand out for the audience, along with other answers as deemed necessary for your organisation.

It is also worth considering the method of communication which you will adopt for the presentation. This undoubtedly will be influenced by the availability of different methods, your own expertise, time and cost. However, consider what method will best present the information and message you want to convey.

Personal presentation of proposals, if done well, is often more effective than remote communications (such as reports), for a number of reasons:

- It makes the process more personal, helping to build relationships
- It offers the chance to stress key points and issues, and to put across enthusiasm for the project
- It allows for explanation and clarification immediately for the audience, to the necessary level
- It increases the chances of having the attention of the people you want to reach
- Feedback and input are immediate
- It allows discussion and debate over feedback and input
- Group dynamics can facilitate more constructive and concise input
- The preparation of the proposal can be less time-consuming, for much of the explanation can be delivered orally.

Remote communications offer some advantages in that they:

- Can be more cost effective
- Allow you to present more detail and supporting evidence
- Do not demand time from the audience in such a rigid manner
- Allow simultaneous access to a geographically spread audience
- Do not require so much arranging and organisation
- Present a consistent message
- Can reduce delays in the presentation of the proposal for approval.

The outputs from stages 2.3.1, 2.3.2 and 2.3.3 will form the core of any proposal to top management. Presenting this information in a clear and concise format will undoubtedly assist in the process, but also think about innovative ways of presenting the information to add impact to specific points or issues.

Depending upon the level of awareness of environmental management and business-related issues, EPE and international standards, it might well be necessary to provide some background and contextual information as part of the proposal. The information in sections 2.1 and 2.2 may well assist in developing this element of the presentation.

Note that it is unlikely at this stage that commitment to and allocation of resources for the entire project will be forthcoming, so the goal should be to secure enough commitment and resources to reach the next milestone or to provide a more extensively researched and detailed project proposal.

Finally, remember that the aim of the proposal is to secure initial commitment to progress with the project. Seek to secure commitment (or to establish a date by which to receive a decision) at the time if possible, in order to maintain the momentum.

2.3.3.4 Arranging to communicate or present to top management

The style of presentation or communication decided upon, and the method chosen, will influence the resources (e.g. facilities, equipment, materials and support) you will require. The following list identifies some guidelines when making arrangements.

- Identify requirements early
- Ensure that intended members of the audience are available, and make arrangements well in advance – this is particularly important for senior managers, larger audiences or where individuals are geographically spread
- Decide upon a location that will suit all intended members of the audience
- Arrange resources well in advance (especially when specialist equipment, materials or support is required)
- Assess whether any delays in communicating or presenting will impact on other elements of the outline plan schedule
- Provide information to attendees on the nature and content of any presentation, allowing preparation and pre-empting contentious situations
- Do not provide excessive amounts of pre-information as this can switch attendees off and/or detract from the impact of your message.

2.3.4 Securing initial management commitment

The principal outputs from this stage will be:

○ Presenting the outline project proposal to top management

○ Obtaining feedback and evaluating the level of commitment secured

○ Identification of further activity required to secure real top mangement commitment

○ Agreement of the outline proposal and of resource requirements

○ List of commitments made and conditions agreed

2.3.4.1 Presenting to top management

In presenting to top management, you should not lose sight of the fact that you are looking for commitment to take the project forward. In order to achieve this, it is possible that you might have to compromise on original plans and timescales, or settle for commitment to progress to a closer milestone.

Maintain the focus on the tangible benefits that the organisation as a whole will derive from the project, ensuring that these are not undermined by any compromises or conditions that you agree in order to secure commitment.

2.3.4.2 Obtaining feedback and evaluating the level of commitment secured

Having made your proposal to top management, you should seek feedback and input into the plans developed. This, potentially, will provide you with additional information and insight, while getting top management involved and giving them the opportunity to shape the process. Ultimately, real commitment will require a certain level of involvement, so achieving that at an early stage is likely to give the project more impetus.

Although commitment may be forthcoming when you present the project proposal, it is worth evaluating how sincere this commitment really is. It is possible that key management members or groups, will want to be seen to be supportive in the presence of superiors or peers yet in reality have little interest in the project, or intention of fulfilling commitments made.

This step of the process will very much be shaped around your own perceptions and instincts, and as such some of your evaluations may well prove to be incorrect. However, failure to recognise when real commitment has not been secured can undermine management efforts, plans and, potentially, the project as whole.

2.3.4.3 Identification of further activity required to secure real commitment

Having evaluated the level of commitment secured from top management representatives and groups, it will be necessary to plan additional activity where requested, and where a lack of real commitment is suspected.

The nature of any such activity will vary from organisation to organisation, and plan to plan, and can only be decided by you based on the nature of the circumstances.

Some examples of additional activity may be:

- To conduct further research
- To develop more-detailed plans
- To review resource requirements
- To make alterations to accommodate specific requirements of top management
- To solicit greater involvement and invite input into the project in order to build ownership
- To re-focus or alter the project proposal better to emphasise the benefits which apply to the parties in question
- To meet or present on a 'one to one' basis with less committed individuals or groups
- To apply pressure, directly or indirectly, on less committed parties, which will test commitments already made.

2.3.4.4 Agreement of the outline plan and of resource requirements

Once actions have been taken (or committed to) to address any requirements of top management, you will be in a position to get agreement for the provision of identified resources and to progress with the project plan.

It is worth noting, however, that some actions related to securing real commitment will be longer term activities. Progress with the project plan should only be undertaken when you are confident that any lack of commitment will not hinder the project too greatly.

Agreement on the outline plan and resource requirements (definite or in principle), must be secured before the project is progressed.

2.3.4.5 List of commitments made and conditions agreed

In securing commitment and agreement to project plans and resources, it is possible that you, as the project initiator, will have had to make some commitments, and agree some conditions. Any such commitment or conditions will, in many cases, shape the nature of EPE and/or the development, implementation and operation of the system.

It is important clearly to record any such commitments and conditions agreed at this early stage, for future reference not only by yourself but by core EPE team members and succeeding project managers or owners. This record can be added to and amended as necessary, at later stages of the process.

The record kept could be in the form of meeting minutes, meeting notes, records of communications (hard copy or electronic) or a bespoke document suited to your project approach.

2.3.5 Establishing the 'core EPE team'

The principal outputs from this stage will be:

○ Identification and appointment of the project manager

○ Identification of a team structure, and format for the functioning of the team

○ Identification of the potential members of the core EPE team(s)

○ To gain commitment from potential members and their superiors

○ To identify skills and information required, against skills and knowledge possessed, among the team (training needs analysis)

○ To plan, arrange and deliver training to provide skills, knowledge and understanding

2.3.5.1 Identifying and appointing a project manager

In order to ensure continuity through project implementation and operation it will be preferable to establish a project manager who will take responsibility and ownership of the project. While this could well be the project initiator, this might not be appropriate in some instances.

In identifying the project manager, you should look for:

- Good project-management skills
- Strong communication skills at all levels
- Commitment to the project
- Ability to commit a sufficient amount of time
- Some insight and understanding of environmental issues and management.

Depending on the nature of the ISO14031 EPE project, other attributes may also be important.

2.3.5.2 Identifying 'core EPE team' structure and format

Given the diverse and cross-functional nature of most EPE activity, the involvement of a wide cross-section of parties in the development, implementation and operation of an EPE system will generally help in making it successful. To channel this involvement in a structured and constructive way, the formulation of a 'core EPE team' or 'teams' can prove highly effective.

However, the availability of potential team members may well be restricted, so the appointment of a core EPE team or teams may not always be practicable. In such cases, greater effort will be required from the project manager in communicating with, and building relationships with, the various interested parties.

In developing the outline project plan and resource requirements in section 2.3.3, you may well have identified the need for a core EPE team or teams and also have identified potential members. In this case, it will be advisable to review these plans, in light of gaining initial top management commitment, and against the considerations highlighted in this stage (if not already done so), before progressing to the next section.

Further to this, it is possible that environmental teams exist already, as a result of other environmental management activity and initiatives, which would be suitable for carrying forward the ISO14031 project.

Initially it may be most suitable to identify a single team, with a view to creating more teams as the need arises at different phases of the project. Where knowledge and planning are limited, beyond initial activity, this is likely to the only sensible approach.

Identifying core EPE team requirements throughout the duration of the project, though, will allow for more accurate resource prediction, early involvement of a wider group of individuals, and the ability to implement initial knowledge and skill building activity ahead of requirements. This will potentially speed up the project process.

Whatever the initial approach, the considerations expressed in this stage are worth noting for future reference.

Where a number of teams have been identified as necessary (for instance, in a large multi site organisation), it is advisable to develop a structure for the teams which defines their role and reporting lines. It is also advisable to establish a format for core EPE team activity, especially when a large number of teams are involved, to provide a common reference point and ensure the focus is maintained.

In the event that you will need to identify a core EPE team or teams, it will be necessary to define the role and structure of the team first.

As there are a number of different stages involved in the overall implementation of the EPE system, and implementation requirements will be likely to differ from operational requirements, it might be most appropriate to identify core EPE teams at different stages.

In this scenario, the core EPE team members could change through the development and implementation of the project, according to skills and knowledge possessed. Take care, however, if taking this approach, not to disillusion and de-motivate team members. In addition, do not underestimate the value of continuity.

Figure 10   Illustrates different approaches to defining the role (or scope) of the core EPE team

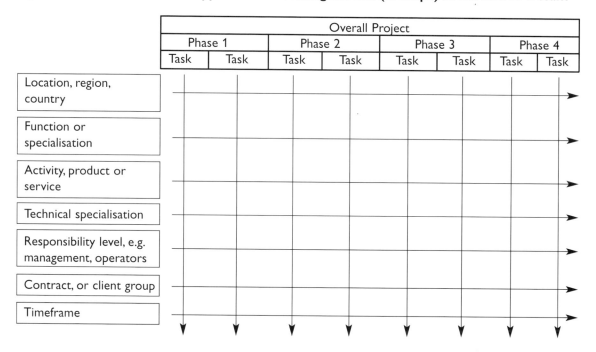

Identifying the role or scope of each core EPE team will begin to help you define the reporting structures between teams.

For example, the creation of teams in different operational locations to see the whole project through may well require the establishment of a central team which is responsible for co-ordinating all locational team activity. Figure 10 illustrates different approaches to defining core EPE team roles.

Co-ordinating teams can be made up of representatives of the 'sub-teams', but beware of the additional time-resource implications of creating too many levels, not to mention the extension of timescales commonly created by greater numbers of reporting levels.

In addition to defining the structure of project teams, it will be necessary to define the internal team-reporting structure. Again, simplicity is the key here, as complex reporting structures and varying levels of authority can hinder the ability of the team to progress action points. Similarly, a lack of leadership and of clearly defined responsibility, or the existence of too many direct participants, can restrict the effectiveness of the team.

Figure 11 illustrates an example of a simple team structure

Figure 11   An example of a simple team structure

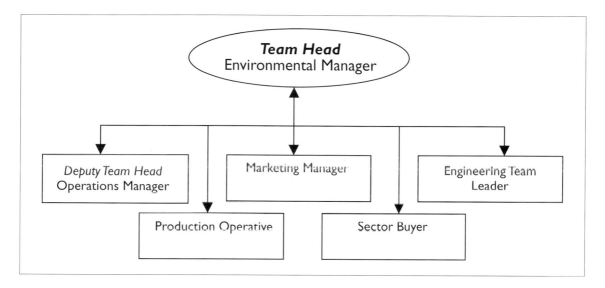

In order to provide consistency of approach and focus for the core EPE team or teams, it can prove useful to develop a standard format for meetings, reporting and approving actions which applies to all teams. This is potentially more applicable where a number of core EPE teams are envisaged, as it is less likely that the project manager will be able to attend all meetings on a routine basis.

A standard format for a core EPE team may stipulate:

- Frequency of team meetings
- A standard agenda
- A standard format for recording meetings
- The reporting structure of the team
- Reporting requirements for the team and individual members
- Targets for teams (e.g. percentage attendance record, percentage actions completed to time scale), and individuals
- Location(s) for meetings

2.3.5.3 Identifying potential 'core EPE team' members

The identification of potential 'core EPE team' members needs to take into account the role and scope of the core EPE team, as well as any requirements for a team head, a deputy or specialist input. Some considerations when selecting team members are provided in Figure 12.

Figure 12 **Considerations when selecting core EPE team members**

Consideration	Notes
Availability	Check whether potential team members can make time or be made available to fulfil their required role.
Competencies	Check that potential team members possess skills and capabilities which will support the role of the team.
Specialist knowledge	Identify individuals who can bring specialist knowledge required by the team.
Experience	Identify individuals that can bring valuable experience (e.g. previous core EPE team members).
Access to resources	Identify individuals who can bring access to resources (e.g. finance, facilities, equipment, materials, labour, specialist skills).
Development potential	Check that potential members show potential for learning and developing (especially if they do not possess necessary skills and knowledge already).
Commitment and enthusiasm	Try to select team members who will be committed and enthusiastic, and who have an interest in making the project a success.
Compatibility with other team members	Check that the potential members bring skills and capabilities, which are complementary. Also, try to select members who can work together effectively.
Level of influence over key individuals or groups	Identify individuals who can influence key individuals or groups (e.g. employee representatives, accountants, senior managers, major investors).
Cost and time	Establish the cost of having certain individuals as team members (e.g. advisers, consultants, contractors, suppliers). Also consider the cost and time implications of involving individuals who will require training supervision and coaching.

Core EPE team membership need not be restricted to employees of the organisation. However, issues related to cost, continuity, conflict of interests and employee motivation need to be assessed against the value which external parties can add.

2.3.5.4 Gaining commitment from potential 'core EPE team' members and their superiors

Once potential 'core EPE team' members have been identified it will be important to gain their commitment, and the commitment of their superiors where appropriate.

Requesting managers to establish teams within their areas can be an effective way of gaining buy-in from superiors, and can overcome the difficulty of assessing individuals unknown to you. However, retaining some control over team membership is likely to be necessary, to ensure that the most effective team is created.

Similarly, requesting volunteers provides members who are motivated to undertake the role, but management approval will be required, and some vetting of volunteers will need to be performed.

The outline plans agreed in stage 2.3.4 will provide a good basis for communicating with and presenting to would-be team members in order to raise awareness and gain commitment, but more-individual approaches may prove more effective. As with top management commitment, it will be valuable to assess whether real commitment has been secured from potential team members and their superiors, and/or whether there are any hidden motives behind commitment which could threaten the project.

2.3.5.5 Identifying skills and information requirements

In section 2.3.5.3, we looked at considerations when selecting team members. Among the considerations outlined in Figure 12, was the identification of existing competencies which would support or complement the role of the team and those of other team members.

When compared with skill and information requirements for enabling the core EPE team to be effective, this will highlight where training, knowledge building and awareness raising will be required.

Appendix 4 provides a template which can be used to record specific and general requirements, against team members' current skills and knowledge.

2.3.5.6 Building skills and knowledge

Starting from the skills and information requirements identified in section 2.3.5.5, it will be necessary to plan training and knowledge-building activity in order to enable the team member sufficiently to contribute to the project and meet established timescales.

Depending upon the team members selected and the subsequent level of instruction and training required, so the timescales and resource projections for the project may need reviewing, and re-approving.

In planning this activity, consideration will need to be given to:

- Availability of team members
- Availability of trainers and communicators
- Research and preparation of training material and information
- Availability of suitable facilities, materials and equipment
- The cost and duration of any activity, and availability of funding
- The urgency for providing a particular element of training or information.

The training and knowledge-building activity can be planned using the template shown in Appendix 5. A summary of this information can be added to the agreed outline plan from section 2.3.4 (originally developed in section 2.3.2). This will enable you to assess whether any of the original timescales will be affected by training timings. If this is the case then you might have to consider bringing training forward or moving task completion dates back, if insufficient flexibility exists in the original plan.

Section 2 checklist

Before you embark on the next stages of EPE implementation you should have:

○　Secured real top management commitment

○　An agreed outline plan of timescales, resource requirements and milestones for the project (or at least the next stages of the project)

○　A vision of what you want the ISO14031 EPE to achieve for the organisation

○　Appointed a project manager

○　Established a core EPE team or teams

○　A plan for delivering training and information to core EPE team members in line with project timescales

○　An understanding of EPE ISO14031 and the relationship with other environmental management tools and standards.

Chapter 3 **Plan: Planning EPE**

By the end of this chapter you should have covered and understood the main requirements for planning an EPE system in line with ISO14031. By following the tasks outlined under each stage you will have developed a plan for implementing and operating an EPE system matched to the needs of your organisation.

The principal outputs from this chapter will be:

- An understanding of the key environmental issues and pressures facing your organisation
  - The identification of significant environmental aspects and impacts
  - The identification of your organisation's environmental performance criteria
  - The evaluation of the views, interests and expectations of interested parties
  - The identification of relevant legislation and regulation and future trends
  - The identification of environmental costs, benefits, and opportunities.
- An understanding of features of your organisation which will influence the development of an EPE system
  - The examination of existing practices and procedures
  - The structure of your organisation
  - The culture of your organisation
  - The identification of potential barriers and opportunities.
- The development of clear goals for the EPE project
- The securing of management commitment
- The selection and development of indicators
- The production of an implementation plan
- The production of an outline operational plan
- The gaining of final approval and commitment

Task Heading	**Understanding the key environmental issues and pressures**
Section Reference	**3.1**
Duration	5 man days +
Difficulty Rating	3
Aims & Objectives	The aim of this section is to develop a clear understanding of the most significant environmental issues and pressures facing your organisation, now and in the foreseeable future. By following each stage in this section you will be able to identify the issues and pressures which need addressing through the EPE system and environmental management.
Outputs	The principal outputs of this section will be: • The identification of relevant legislation and regulation and future trends • The identification of your organisation's environmental performance criteria • The evaluation of the views, interests and expectations of interested parties • The identification of environmental costs, benefits, and opportunities • The identification of significant environmental aspects and impacts.
Resource Considerations	
People	Project manager Core EPE team Top management Functional management Operational management Supervisory staff Operational staff Advisers and consultants
Physical	Work station and office facilities Meeting facilities Access to information Transport and communications Commercial tools and packages (software based or hard copy)
Outputs from Previous Tasks	• An outline plan with timescales and milestones for developing an EPE system. Section 2.3.2 • An outline of initial resource requirements to achieve the first milestone. Section 2.3.3 • Initial top management commitment. Section 2.3.4
Potential Problems	• Lack of competencies within core EPE team • Lack of necessary resources • Lack of real commitment at key management levels • Limited availability of information required to gain strong understanding • Over complicating significance assessment processes • Limited range of input or consultation

Potential Opportunities	• Identification of threats and opportunities to be addressed by the organisation.
	• Identification of key interested parties and the development of relationships (internally and externally)
	• Raising awareness of environmental issues within the organisation
	• Development of a platform for building knowledge and understanding through the organisation and beyond.

The stages outlined in this section include guidance for the assessment of key environmental issues and pressures facing your organisation. In some of the stages the guidance extends to cover techniques which could be applied in more complex or wide-ranging circumstances. You should be aware that these techniques can be simplified for less involved applications.

3.1.1 Environmental legislation and regulation

The principal outputs from this stage will be:

O   The identification of all relevant environmental legislative requirements

O   The review of trends in the enforcement of environmental legislation applicable to your organisation

O   The identification of relevant proposed legislation which is under development

O   The appraisal of future legislative trends

O   The consideration of voluntary schemes and codes of practice

O   The preparation of a summary of all relevant legislative (and voluntary) requirements, developments, exposure and opportunites.

Environmental legislation and regulation is commonly one of the most potent drivers for environmental activity within organisations, given the potential repercussions of non-compliance. In view of this, the existence of legislation will have a major influence on the assessment of significance. Further to this, the establishment of the organisation's environmental criteria, and the assessment of the views of interested parties (to be discussed in the following sections), will require an understanding of legislative and regulatory requirements.

The volume and variety of environmental legislation is ever increasing, and with this the interpretation, level and severity of enforcement activity are also changing. In view of this, it is important to:

• Identify and review continuously the legislative requirements which apply to your organisation
• Track enforcement trends, official interpretations and penalties awarded with regard to each relevant piece of legislation

- Identify future legislation under development
- Identify future legislative trends.

3.1.1.1 Identifying legislation which applies to your organisation

This can be done through the use of a number of tools and sources:

- 'Off-the shelf' legislation packages (normally software-based), such as Technical Index, CEDREC or Croners electronic. These systems allow you quickly to assess both legislation and case law on issues, processes or substances. They can allow you to develop an outline of legislative requirements quickly and easily. However, they do not allow you to consider other requirements such as voluntary schemes or local commitments
- Environmental legislation bulletins, as published by Croners, GEE (most of these publications provide regular updates and guidance on interpretation)
- Internal management and responsible operators. If the responsibility for environmental management has traditionally been at functional or divisional level it is likely that some level of understanding already exists
- Enforcement bodies, e.g. Environment Agency (EA) or Scottish Environment Protection Agency (SEPA), local authority (for UK). Opening dialogue with enforcement agencies is commonly resisted, but in most cases this initiative will be viewed positively, provides definitive guidance on interpretation, and starts to build a relationship with key interested parties
- Trade and industry associations' publications and services. The availability and quality of information provided through these channels varies considerably from industry to industry, but as awareness and interest increase it is likely that this will become an increasingly rich source of information and guidance
- Environmental legal specialists. Not a cheap option, but can add value in complex, ambiguous or controversial circumstances. The level of competence and resource within the organisation will also have bearing on the value which such specialists can contribute.

3.1.1.2 The tracking of enforcement trends

Enforcement trends, legal precedents, official interpretations and penalties awarded can be tracked through the use of all the sources mentioned above. In addition to this, there are many environmental news services, such as ENDS, who provide regular reports on environmental legislative issues and prosecutions at local, national and international level.

3.1.1.3 Identifying future legislation under development

This can be achieved through the use of all the information sources mentioned above. Legal developments in the UK usually follow from European Union Directives, though the exact mechanics of the legislation will tend to vary from member state to member state. Legislation can originate independently from UK government departments, although this is becoming less common, and when it does lengthy consultation processes are normally applied. Monitoring government information and bulletins will also alert you to any current or forthcoming consultation processes.

3.1.1.4 The identification of legislative trends

While inevitably imprecise and open to subjectivity, the identification of legislative trends is an important part of any environmental strategy development. Environmental news services will often provide objective comment on predicted trends more readily than other bodies. Environmental pressure groups and lobbyists are further sources by which to gauge possible trends, but any such information needs to be evaluated carefully.

3.1.1.5 The consideration of voluntary schemes and codes of practice

It is possible that your organisation subscribes on a voluntary basis to agreements, protocols or codes of practice which are outside the legal framework. In such cases, the requirements of these should be treated in a similar manner to legal requirements, albeit that the sources of information may well be more limited or restricted.

With voluntary schemes, it is important to assess the liabilities faced in the event of a breach or of pulling out. The extent of the liability will depend on the support and profile of the scheme, and the power of the supporting body or parties. In some industries, voluntary schemes have proved to be more powerful incentives for positive activity than legislative measures, given the commercial damage which can be inflicted by failure to subscribe and comply.

Examples of successful and influential voluntary environmental schemes include Responsible Care, within the chemical industry, and the Forestry Stewardship Council (FSC), within the timber and related products sector.

3.1.1.6 Preparing a summary of all relevant legislative (and voluntary) requirements

From the information gathered in this stage, it will be useful to prepare a summary detailing the relevant current legislation and voluntary schemes, and the areas of your operation where they apply. In addition, you can prepare a similar summary for likely legislative developments.

Once you have identified activities, products and services which are, or are likely to be, covered by environmental legislation, you should estimate the degree of control that is exerted over these areas to ensure legal compliance. This will identify the level of risk of legal action faced by your organisation. Auditing your activities, products or services against legislative requirements is a common approach used to assess the current position and gauge the level of control exerted.

Conversely, it is worth identifying any opportunities which might be presented to your organisation through existing or forthcoming legislation.

3.1.2 Organisation environmental performance criteria

The principal outputs from this stage will be:

O   The identification of stated environmental performance criteria for the organisation

O   The appraisal of top management aspirations and expectations

O   The identification of environmental performance criteria applied or envisaged at lower levels within the organisation

O   The preparation of a summary prioritising existing and proposed environmental performance criteria with supporting information

The development of an EPE system should incorporate the identification and/or establishment of environmental performance criteria, against which performance can be compared and analysed.

Environmental performance criteria are defined in ISO14031 as 'environmental objectives, targets, or other intended levels of performance, set by the management of the organisation, and used for the purpose of environmental performance evaluation'.

Most organisations will already have established environmental performance criteria, to a greater or lesser degree. But unless the organisation has already embarked on some form of environmental management activity, it is likely that such performance criteria are not specifically identified as being 'environmental'.

For example, the majority of organisations' top management will expect their representatives to act in accordance with relevant environmental legislation and regulation. This requirement may well be bracketed under a performance criteria which is 'to ensure compliance with relevant legislation at all times'.

In contrast to this, some stated environmental performance criteria are not actively supported, or are interpreted in different ways across the organisation. It is important to note any characteristics of criteria during the identification and appraisal steps.

3.1.2.1 Identifying stated environmental performance criteria

The number and intensity of environmental performance criteria, if they exist, will vary from one organisation to another, depending on a range of variables. For example:

* The nature of the organisation's activities, products or services
* The level of environmental awareness at senior management levels
* The extent of environmental engagement of the organisation
* The values and beliefs of owners, founders, investors or current management
* The perceived level of risks to the organisation from environmental issues
* Historical experience with environmental issues
* The extent to which the organisation's reputation, products or services are based on environmental credentials
* The views of interested parties (see section 3.1.3).

Information about your organisation's environmental performance criteria, if unclear, can be obtained through a number of methods:

* Objectives and targets established as part of an EMS or other environmental initiative
* Internal communications, programmes and initiatives
* Public statements, reports
* Requirements under voluntary agreements or sector codes of practice
* Interviews with relevant managers or key personnel
* Questionnaires and surveys of managers or key personnel
* Multi-functional team meetings/workshops.

The most suitable methods to adopt will depend on the scale, complexity and culture of your organisation. The list above is roughly in order of how time-consuming each method is likely to be. Criteria identified can be recorded using the template provided in Appendix 6 and there is also space provided to make any notes relating to the nature, application and reporting for each criterion.

3.1.2.2   Appraising the aspirations and expectations of top management

It is worth remembering that environmental performance criteria may not always be obvious, owing to the way they are classified and/or communicated through the organisation. Appraising the expectations and aspirations of top management may be a necessary first step in identifying key criteria.

3.1.2.3   Identifying environmental performance criteria at lower levels within the organisation

In addition to this it is worth noting that environmental performance criteria may well exist (and be driven) at a lower level in the organisation, officially or unofficially. For example, a supervisor who has responsibility for purchasing low value consumables may be required to apply some environmental criteria (e.g. good product durability, supplier packaging takeback scheme) by management. In addition, however, the supervisor may also apply criteria of his own (e.g. will not buy from suppliers whose containers make handling difficult and increase the chances of spillages, or buys products with the highest amount of recycled content).

Criteria may also be applied independently by subsidiary companies, divisions, functions, departments, facilities, teams and even individuals. Knowledge of any such criteria (official or unofficial) is important in order that they can be accounted for when establishing criteria for the EPE system. This is not to say that they will necessarily be incorporated, but knowledge allows for potential conflicts to be identified in advance and cultural issues to be addressed.

3.1.2.4   Summarising and prioritising criteria

Having identified the environmental performance criteria applied within the organisation and further, anticipated criteria, it will be useful if you summarise this information, prioritising the criteria in terms of their importance within the organisation. For example, legal compliance criteria will probably be more important than criteria on waste minimisation and involvement in community projects. Appendix 6 can used to present this summary.

While it is likely that existing criteria will rank as most important, it is possible that anticipated criteria could also be important, especially if they represent a response to sudden and unexpected pressures or new legislation.

Furthermore, criteria which are not currently being observed by management or other groups within the organisation may also require high priority. For example, an environmental criterion of the organisation might be to check on a weekly basis that spill kits are in place and usable, but in practice it may be that these are only checked monthly, in the health and safety site inspections.

In addition to prioritising the criteria, it would also be useful to identify those criteria which are out of date or unsuitable for the organisation, and which you will seek to remove in the development of the EPE system. This is most likely to apply to some criteria applied at lower levels of the organisation.

Finally, in summarising the information collated it is worth adding against criteria any notes which will provide useful context.

3.1.3 Views of interested parties

> The principal outputs from this stage will be:
>
> O   Identify potential interested parties
>
> O   Outline the likely views, issues of concern and expectations of these interested parties
>
> O   Evaluate stragetic significance of the interested parties
>
> O   Evaluate the strategic significance of likely views, issues and expectations
>
> O   Find out the views of key interested parties
>
> O   Re-evaluate views, issues and expectations, and summarise.

The term 'interested parties' (or 'stakeholders') covers a wide range of groups, official bodies and individuals, all with differing relationships to the organisation, as well as different interests and objectives, levels of influence and levels of exposure.

ISO14031 defines an interested party as an 'individual or group concerned with or affected by the environmental performance of the organisation'.

Figure 13 identifies a number of potential parties who might have an interest in the environmental activities of the organisation. This diagram is intended for illustrative purposes and is not an exhaustive list. In the majority of cases all of the interested parties within the organisation will be important (in particular, owners, management and employees), whereas the extent to which external interested parties are important will vary considerably.

Figure 13 **Potential interested parties**

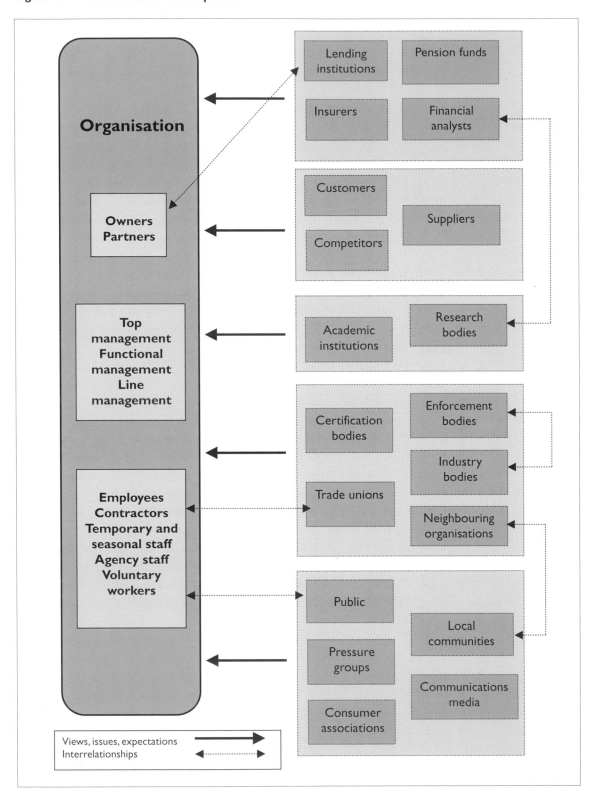

Given the different perspectives and objectives of the various interested parties, the expectations for the organisation will differ from party to party. In a number of cases these expectations may conflict with one another. In order to decide on actions that best serve the organisation as a whole, it will be necessary to identify:

* Who the interested parties are
* What issues they view as most important
* How influential they are
* How active they are.

This will lead to the identification of the key, or strategically significant, interested parties. The following stages look at the identification of key interested parties for the more-complex situations. However, it is possible to identify these interested parties at a brainstorming level, addressing the four points mentioned above. Whichever approach is adopted, Appendix 7 might prove useful for recording the output from this stage. It is designed for information to be recorded under the stages of this section, but if a brainstorming approach is being applied then some of the columns can be left blank or used for alternative information.

3.1.3.1 Identifying potential interested parties

This identification of potential interested parties can be carried out as a desk-top exercise, though it may be useful to involve a range of key personnel from within the organisation. The strategic importance of the interested parties does not need to be assessed at this stage, so include all potentials.

3.1.3.2 Outlining likely views

Again, this step can be carried out as a desk-top exercise. Consideration needs to be given to issues of concern and the expectations of the interested parties. The perceptions of different stakeholder groups will be an important factor to consider here, as issues will take on different significance with different interpretations and levels of knowledge and understanding.

At this stage it might be possible to obtain direct input from interested parties with whom strong relationships exist. However, consideration needs to be given to the sensitivity of the issues and of interested parties, as poorly prepared or unnecessary communications may only provoke reaction and end up being counter-productive.

3.1.3.3   Evaluating strategic significance of interested parties

Of the various interested parties identified under stage one (section 3.1.3.1), each will have a different strategic significance for your organisation. This will be dependent upon how much they can impact on your organisation – that is, upon the level of influence they can exert (directly or indirectly) and how active they are in utilising any power or influence.

For example, investors in the organisation may be viewed as having greater influence than an industry trade association, and therefore be seen as strategically more important.

However, if a principal investor uses the trade association to conduct research on its behalf and produce benchmarking information on environmental performance, the influence of the trade association may well be increased. In this scenario the importance of recognising interrelationships between interested parties can be seen. In some cases strong interrelationships can elevate otherwise insignificant interested parties into very significant positions.

The strategic importance of an interested party to the organisation will also be dictated by how active the party is in exerting influence.

For example, until recently local community action on environmental issues has tended to be low key, as a result of a lack of knowledge, understanding, resources, rights and organisation within the community. As a community, the level of influence that can be exerted directly and through local and national government is potentially very significant, yet the barriers identified above have tended to make local communities dormant. In the case of local communities, particularly in developed countries, the barriers are beginning to come down, and consequently activity and the influence being brought to bear are increasing.

Identifying the strategically significant interested parties will help in deciding which parties to open up dialogue with and foster goodwill with, and which issues to focus environmental management effort on.

> ### Case example   The WWF 95+ Group: applying influence through indirect relationships to change forestry practices
>
> *The World Wide Fund for Nature (WWF) is a globally active environmental pressure group in the area of forestry and timber related products.*

The strategic significance of interested parties can be rated using a variety of scoring or colour-coding schemes, as deemed most suitable. However, if this approach is adopted, it is advisable to keep the systems simple, such as high, medium, low, 1,2,3, or red, amber, green, as a large amount of detailed analysis is unnecessary here.

To assist interpretation and the checking of the results, it is also advisable to make a note of the key reasons for identifying an interested party as strategically significant, whether the interested party is directly or indirectly significant and how active the interested party is believed to be.

3.1.3.4   Evaluating the strategic significance of likely views

The likely significance of an interested party will undoubtedly tend to focus the organisation on the issues of concern to that party, but it does not always follow that the most strategically significant interested party is interested in the most strategically significant issues. For this reason it is important to evaluate the views and issues on their own merits.

When assessing strategic significance there is a tendency to focus on risks or threats to the organisation. However, it is equally important to consider opportunities. For example, not addressing environmental issues has the potential to lead to a loss of orders or contracts, while on the other hand a proactive approach to these issues ahead of the competition could well win favour with the customer as well as raising the stakes for competitors.

If you choose to rate the significance of issues, apply the same principles as outlined in section 3.1.3.3. Similarly, note the reasons for having identified issues as strategically significant.

3.1.3.5 Find out the views of key interested parties

Where strong relationships exist between the organisation and an interested party, it will be valuable to identify the views of the interested party directly, in order to support the process. In many cases though, the relationships with key interested parties are not strong, and are sometimes adversarial. Furthermore, interested parties who are dormant may well be activated as a result of being approached for their viewpoint, alerting them to issues which may or may not exist.

It will be necessary carefully to consider any approaches made to these interested parties and the benefits which you perceive being able to derive. Consideration also needs to be given to other objectives of the organisation, and it is often advisable to gain widespread approval for any advances to interested parties.

You will need to consider whether to try to discover the views of interested parties in a direct manner or through secondary sources. Both approaches have their advantages, but also their drawbacks, especially if applied with little consideration or planning, and the type of approach needs to be selected on a case by case basis. Figure 14 identifies some techniques for identifying the views of interested parties.

Direct techniques will generally provide information of a higher level of quality and detail, and will allow for the development of relationships with the interested parties. However, direct techniques will tend to be more resource intensive than secondary methods, and offer little or no anonymity.

3.1.3.6 Re-evaluate views, issues and expectations, and summarise

From feedback and information received on the views of interested parties the findings under stages 3.1.3.2 to 3.1.3.4 will need to be reviewed and altered where necessary.

With this updated information it will be possible to identify and summarise the most important interested parties and issues.

Mapping the key interested parties and issues can assist in preparing this summary. Figure 15 gives an example of how this can be done. The visual impact of such mapping diagrams can be enhanced with the use of colour. For example: red = high strategic significance; amber = moderate; green = low. And the width of the connecting arrows can be altered to indicate the strength of the relationship or feeling about an issue.

Figure 14 Techniques for identifying the views of interested parties

Direct Techniques	Advantages	Disadvantages
Direct surveys and questionnaires	Relatively low cost and time implications. Particularly effective for reaching large and dispersed groups. Offers a consistency of approach.	Forms need careful design. Responses may not be secured from all parties approached. Can highlight sensitive issues and raise false expectations. Can be a lengthy process. Potential for misinterpretation of questions and responses.
Employee suggestions	Low cost and resource implications. Effective for reaching large numbers and/or dispersed employees.	Commonly poor response rate. Can raise false expectations. Slow response time.
Meetings and workshops, and forums	Immediate response. Opportunity to share knowledge and build relationships. Chance to clarify intentions. Enhances the profile of the exercise.	Time consuming and sometimes costly. Difficult to get all required parties together at once. Skilled facilitators are required to get the most from the process. Delegates might expect follow-up activity.
Interviews	Immediate response from interviewee. Opportunity to share knowledge and build relationships. Chance to clarify intentions. Exercise becomes high profile for interviewee. Option to be more flexible in approach to obtaining information.	Very time consuming and potentially costly. Unsuitable for large groups. Slower response time overall. Heavily reliant on the interviewer's ability and interpretation of responses.

Direct Techniques	Advantages	Disadvantages
Participation in industry and public interest groups	Demonstrates commitment. Opportunity to share knowledge and build relationships. Chance to clarify intentions. Part of ongoing dialogue. Potential exposure to a large range of interested parties at one forum.	Less control over the process and direction. Honest and frank exchange is less likely. Time consuming and potentially slow moving. Can highlight sensitive issues and raise false expectations. Make up of group(s) is possibly an unrepresentative sample.

Secondary Techniques	Advantages	Disadvantages
Review of public statements, brochures, web sites, internal programmes and initiatives of interested parties	Low cost. Relatively quick to collect information. Maintains high level of anonymity.	Information obtained will only be what people want you to know or believe about them. Not all interested parties state their views. Information is potentially dated
Market research	Consistency of approach. Information is up to date.	High cost. Needs careful compilation. Lower level of anonymity.
Regulatory tracking	Low cost and accessible. Maintains high level of anonymity.	Only provides information on legal requirements, not commercial or moral issues.
Information from the media and other sources of public information	Low cost. Relatively quick to collect information. Maintains high level of anonymity.	Will not cover all views or issues. Information may be subjective or inaccurate. Information is potentially dated.
Voluntary guidelines and standards	Low cost (though information may have to be paid for). Clearly defines criteria and intent. Possible to remain anonymous.	Non-subscribers may not be non-believers. Information potentially inaccessible and may be dated. Tend only to apply to formal organisations or groups.

Figure 15   Example of mapping interested parties and issues

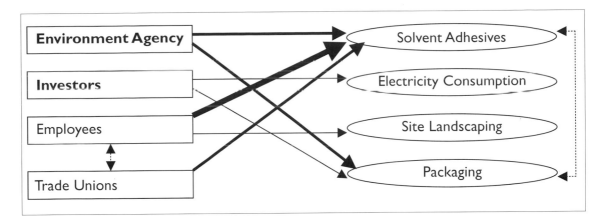

Key:

- Bold text indicates strategic significance
- Line thickness indicates the importance of the environmental issue to the interested party (the thicker the line the higher the importance)
- Dotted connection indicates interrelationship.

3.1.4   Environmental costs and benefits

> The principal outputs from this stage will be:
>
> ○ The identification of financial costs and benefits related to environmental issues, pressures and activities
>
> ○ The identification of non-financial costs and benefits
>
> ○ The summarisation and prioritisation of costs and benefits.

Understanding the nature and extent of environmental costs and benefits is central to the development of an effective EPE system, which will need clearly to define goals and direction. For the most part, goals and direction will be decided upon on the basis of costs and/or benefits, be these real or perceived, tangible or intangible. Top management will certainly want to know what they are going to get in return for their commitment.

Not all costs and benefits are always apparent at the outset of a project, as indeed forecast costs and benefits are not always accurate. However, some evaluation of current, future and potential costs and benefits will be required to give the EPE system, and any EMS activity, a value-adding focus and direction. If the EPE system is to support value-adding goals and direction, indicators will need to be selected and developed which focus on key costs and benefits.

The terms 'costs' and 'benefits' commonly lead us to think about financial valuations. Beyond this, however, many costs and benefits are impractical to value, albeit they are clearly recognised as detrimental or beneficial.

3.1.4.1 Identifying financial costs and benefits

When identifying financial costs and benefits, it will help if you categorise them into one of three categories:

- Costs
- Savings
- Revenues.

Consider the current situation, and the potential or desired future situation. Also assess what proportion of any cost, saving or revenue will be ongoing, as opposed to a one off.

Figure 16 identifies some areas to consider when trying to identify financial costs, savings and revenues within your organisation, and Appendix 8 provides a template for recording this information.

Figure 16 **Considerations when identifying financial costs and benefits**

Financial cost or or benefit	Considerations
Cost	<ul><li>Inputs (e.g. fuel, water, electricity, raw materials, components, ancillary products, services)</li><li>Waste outputs (solid waste, liquid waste, special wastes, effluent discharges, gaseous emissions, heat loss, noise, vibration, light, odours)</li><li>Product and service outputs (materials and time input, packaging, storage, handling, distribution, take back and disposal)</li><li>Facilities and equipment (operational requirements, maintenance, servicing, life expectancy, replacement, resource efficiency, end of life disposal)</li><li>Legal and regulatory compliance (testing, inspections, calibration, recording, reporting, permits, registration, training, provision of protective equipment, provision of emergency equipment and facilities)</li><li>Management and administration (development, implementation and operation of management systems, reporting requirements, problem solving, project work and research, communicating, building and maintaining relationships).</li></ul>

Financial cost or or benefit	Considerations
Savings	• Process design • Product design • Substitute materials or components • Facilities design and layout • Equipment specification and provision • Working practices • Planning and scheduling • Resource utilisation • Material and product flows • Information management and flows • Restrictions('legislative, structural, contractual, cultural, technical, spatial) • Reuse, recycling and recovery.
Revenues	• Recycling and recovery of outputs (selling waste, exporting energy from incineration or processes) • Importation of waste (for reuse, recycling, recovery, treatment) • Take back (of product for reuse, recycling, recovery, treatment) • Sales of managed renewable resources • Consolidating market share by matching competitors, creating opportunities by exceeding competitor standards • Products with strong environmental credentials and image • Products which are efficient in use and disposal • Products which reduce environmental risks for customer or consumer • Provision of services at lower impact to the environment • Service provision to replace product.

If you are identifying actual values at this stage, and can identify improvement projects, it will be worth calculating the payback period, or rate of return on the project, in order to support commitment-gaining activities.

3.1.4.2 Identifying non-financial costs and benefits

Some of the most significant costs and benefits associated with environmental activity cannot be given a definite value (monetary or otherwise).

In identifying non-financial costs and benefits there is a distinction to make between costs and benefits for which a monetary value can be predicted or assumed, and those which warrant evaluation on a purely qualitative basis. This section defines three categories of non-financial costs and benefits to use in identification.

• Risk related
• Perception related
• Qualitative.

Risk related costs and benefits are those which result from an incident or occurrence (or the avoidance of an incident or occurrence). You will need to focus on the costs resulting from the incident or occurrence, but stress the point that these costs (and any benefits), while worthy of consideration, will only accrue in the event that the predicted incident or occurrence happens. Therefore the level of risk (actual or perceived) will determine the perceived values for the organisation.

Some interested parties will consider the impact of environmental performance on the value of the organisation expressed in terms of share value or 'goodwill'. Here, the measurement of hard monetary values is more subjective, and opportunity exists to value financially intangible benefits derived from such activity, such as improving corporate image. Non-commercial organisations may well find that such image-related costs and benefits cannot sensibly be converted into monetary terms, and as such will be listed as qualitative.

Figure 17 identifies some areas to consider when trying to identify non-financial costs and benefits within your organisation. Appendix 8 can also be used for recording this information, albeit that some of the sections will not be relevant.

Figure 17 **Considerations when identifying non-financial costs and benefits.**

Non-financial cost or benefit	Considerations
Risk	• Legal (fines, clean-up costs, damages and compensation, out of court settlements, legal representation and advice) • Insurance costs (pay outs) • Asset damage or loss • Materials and product damage, loss or recall • Plant or facility down time • Damage to corporate image • Damage to brand image • Breach of contract (compensation, loss of contract and/or sales) • Consequential losses • Bad debts • Speculative losses.
Perception	• Publicity • Management effectiveness and control • Risk exposure • Efficiency • Entrepreneurial ability • Flexibility • Innovation • Technology • Industry standing.

Non-financial cost or benefit	Considerations
Qualitative	• Opportunity creation or limitation • Motivational influences • Skills, knowledge and competency building or eroding • Continuity and stability • Strength of relationships • Flexibility • Political positioning • Status, pride and esteem • Fear or security • Promotion of values and beliefs.

It is likely that some of the financial costs and benefits identified under the previous stage will interact with non-financial costs and benefits, either in a complementary manner or as a trade off.

An example of a complementary interaction would be that by increasing recycling activity you reduce product waste costs, and also gain positive publicity for the organisation.

An example of a trade off would be building a bund around your fuel storage tank, which will cost you money but will reduce the risk of a serious pollution incident should the tank develop a leak (and the costs related to that).

Although attaching monetary values to some non-financial costs and benefits may seem inappropriate, doing so (where possible) will often prove useful in supporting project and initiation proposals, as appraisal will often concentrate on the return on investment.

3.1.5 Identification of significant aspects and impacts

The principal outputs from this stage will be:

○ An understanding of the difference between an environmental aspect and an environmental impact

○ An understanding of the different approaches which can be adopted for the assessment of aspect and impact significance

○ The identification of activities, products or services to be assessed

○ The identification of environmental aspects relating to each activity, product or service identified

○	The identification of environmental impacts related to the aspects identified	
○	A significance evaluation of aspects and/or impacts	
○	A prioritised summary of significant environmental asepcts and impacts	

3.1.5.1 Defining aspects and impacts

Environmental aspects and impacts are commonly referred to throughout environmental management following the adoption of these terms by ISO14001 (note that you might find impacts referred to as effects in some instances).

Figure 18 provides the ISO14001 definitions, and further explanation of these terms.

Figure 18 **Definition of aspects and impacts**

Term	As Per	Definition
ASPECT	ISO14001	'An element of an organisation's activities, products or services that can interact with the environment.'
		An environmental aspect has the potential to impact on the environment, but the extent of the impact will vary according to factors within or beyond the control of the organisation.
	Example	Example of an environmental aspect: fuel consumption through the operation of company cars. There are a number of environmental impacts arising from fuel consumption. (Note: fuel consumption is not the only environmental aspect related to the operation of company cars.)
IMPACT	ISO14001	'Any change to the environment, whether adverse or beneficial, wholly or partially resulting from an organisation's activities, products or services.'
		Actual physical change in the environment resulting from an aspect under normal or abnormal conditions.
	Example	Aspect, fuel consumption. Examples of environmental impacts: • Non-renewable resource depletion. • Disruption to habitats and ecosystems through extraction and releases. • Emissions of CO_2 (contribute to global warming), CO (toxic to humans), NO & NO_2 (contribute to acidification, human respiratory problems), VOCs (act as a catalyst for ground ozone creation with NO_2, and contain carcinogens), SO_2 (contribute to acidification and human respiratory problems), particulate matter (cause human respiratory problems, and soiling).

3.1.5.2   **Approaches to assessing significance**

Assessing the significance of aspects and/or impacts enables identification of the most important environmental issues relating to the organisation. Establishing and maintaining procedures for the assessment of the significance of aspects and impacts is a requirement of ISO14001, and ISO14031 suggests[1] the consideration of your significant aspects and impacts as a central element of the planning phase.

Figure 19 provides the ISO14001 definition of significance, and further explanation in the context of the company car fuel use example used in Figure 18.

Figure 19   **Definition of significance**

SIGNIFICANCE	ISO14001	'A significant environmental aspect is an environmental aspect which can have a significant environmental impact.'
		The significance of an environmental impact has to be gauged in relation to the rest of the impacts that an organisation recognises as its responsibility.
		In the absence of accepted scientific evidence, determining the relative significance of different environmental impacts is likely to be based on perception.
		Where other commercial or ethical pressures are brought to bear, significance to the organisation may not be driven solely (if at all) by the extent of change to the environment.
	Example	Aspect, fuel consumption. <ul><li>Is fuel consumption important in relation to other aspects identified? Possible to compare in volume terms, cost, applicability of legal restrictions, perceived risks.</li><li>Which impacts are most significant in environmental terms? Difficult to determine objectively.</li><li>What, if any, commercial or ethical drivers exist to make an impact significant? Possibly, costs savings through fuel efficiency, risk of rising fuel prices, tax breaks for cleaner fuels, fostering employee, local community and pressure group goodwill.</li></ul>

[1] ISO14031 does not specify any formal approach to this, but keeping some record of the approach taken will undoubtedly help at review stages and in ongoing operation of the EPE system.

Significance assessment can be achieved by many different methods, all of which have their strengths and weaknesses. The approach adopted should be suitable for the size and scale of the organisation, as well as the level of information, resources and time available.

The assessment of significance can consider both environmental and commercial angles. The extent of impact on the environment has traditionally driven the significance assessment, but the nature of the environment and a lack of understanding of the complex interactions and relationships within it make determining environmental significance in absolute terms difficult. Commercial pressures (or opportunities) are often more easily defined and quantified, as well as having greater relevance to commercially orientated organisations. Figure 20 identifies five generic commercial drivers which might form the basis for identifying commercial pressures and subsequently significance.

As already mentioned there are many methods of assessing the significance of environmental aspects and impacts. Figure 21 identifies some common methodological approaches, and identifies the principal strengths and weaknesses of each.

It is worth mentioning that not all of the methods mentioned in Figure 21, will meet the requirements of ISO14001, whereas they could prove an appropriate approach under ISO14031.

Given the less rigorous requirements of ISO14031, brainstorming likely significance of environmental aspects and impacts might present a more manageable option initially. Appendix 9 provides a template which could be used to facilitate this process. Taking the less formal, brainstorming approach will reduce the amount of effort and time required for the following stages of this section, but reading through these stages might help prompt some ideas which could improve the results of the assessment.

If you already have an ISO14001 compliant EMS in place, you will have established procedures for assessing significance, and probably completed the assessment of aspects and impacts.

Figure 20 **Five generic commercial drivers of environmental significance**

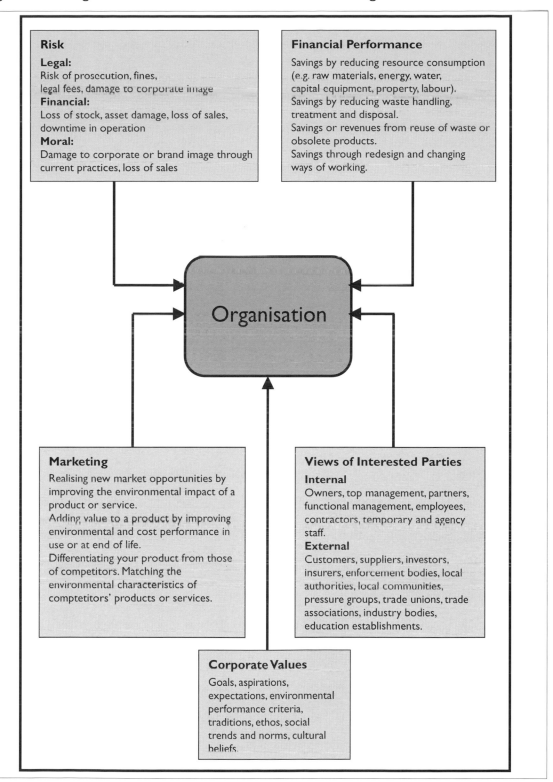

Risk

Legal:
Risk of prosecution, fines,
legal fees, damage to corporate image

Financial:
Loss of stock, asset damage, loss of sales,
downtime in operation

Moral:
Damage to corporate or brand image through
current practices, loss of sales

Financial Performance

Savings by reducing resource consumption
(e.g. raw materials, energy, water,
capital equipment, property, labour).
Savings by reducing waste handling,
treatment and disposal.
Savings or revenues from reuse of waste or
obsolete products.
Savings through redesign and changing
ways of working.

Organisation

Marketing

Realising new market opportunities by
improving the environmental impact of a
product or service.
Adding value to a product by improving
environmental and cost performance in
use or at end of life.
Differentiating your product from those
of competitors. Matching the
environmental characteristics of
comptetitors' products or services.

Views of Interested Parties

Internal
Owners, top management, partners,
functional management, employees,
contractors, temporary and agency
staff.

External
Customers, suppliers, investors,
insurers, enforcement bodies, local
authorities, local communities,
pressure groups, trade unions, trade
associations, industry bodies,
education establishments.

Corporate Values

Goals, aspirations,
expectations, environmental
performance criteria,
traditions, ethos, social
trends and norms, cultural
beliefs.

Figure 21   Different methods for assessing the significance of environmental aspects and impacts.

Environmental impact related scoring	This approach focuses exclusively on the extent of environmental impact and seeks to score the significance of each aspect and/or impact. This approach is suitable for ISO14001, and is one of the most commonly adopted approaches.
Benefits	It maintains focus on the principal purpose of environmental management, to protect and enhance the environment. It can expose areas for concern that were previously unrecognised. Quantifying significance allows for quick assessment and prioritisation of significance. Scoring systems are easy to associate with and support the presentation and communication of information. The impact of actions to address aspects and impacts can be reflected quickly, and in consistent terms. The approach is easy to put into a procedure and meets the requirements of ISO14001.
Drawbacks	Focus is purely on environmental impact, and not on commercial factors, which might lead to the views and expectations of important interested parties being overlooked. The scoring approach for environmental issues is likely to be influenced greatly by perceptions, making it highly subjective. The complex nature of environmental issues, and the relationship between risk and impacts, often make scoring systems highly complex, over bureaucratic, and time consuming. Consistency of scoring is difficult, and will require the creation of scoring rules and results testing. Arbitrary cut-off points are often created when prioritising significant aspects and/or impacts. Scores can hinder understanding of environmental aspects and impacts.
Commercially focused scoring	This approach focuses on the significance of the commercial pressures related to environmental aspects and impacts of the organisation. Scoring is used to identify the significance of each aspect and/or impact, though this can sometimes be related to financial information. This approach would probably need to consider the extent of environmental impact as well, in order to satisfy the requirements of ISO14001.
Benefits	Focuses on issues and pressures of direct importance to the organisation, therefore strengthening arguments when seeking commitment and support. It can expose areas for concern that were previously unrecognised. Quantifying significance allows for quick assessment and prioritisation of significance. Scoring systems are easy to associate with and support the presentation and communication of information.
Drawbacks	Focus is on commercial issues and pressures, which might lead to important environmental aspects and impacts being overlooked. The scoring approach for commercial issues can be influenced by perceptions, albeit that this is less likely than for environmental issues.

Drawbacks: continued	Scoring systems can become highly complex, over bureaucratic, and time consuming.
	Consistency of scoring is difficult, and will require the creation of scoring rules and results testing.
	Arbitrary cut-off points are often created when prioritising significant aspects and/or impacts.
	Scores can hinder a broader understanding of the commercial issues and pressures identified. It might not satisfy ISO14001 requirements without further consideration of environmental aspects and impacts.
Environmental and commercial qualitative assessment	This approach does not attempt to quantify significance but attempts to assess significance in a qualitative manner. The use of colours or symbols can sometimes be applied as opposed to scores, to complement notes and comments. This approach can be suitable for ISO14001, as long as it is clearly defined and consistently applied.
Benefits	Provides a balanced assessment of environmental and commercial issues.
	Allows for a more objective consideration of intangible factors or areas of uncertainty.
	Does away with the need for scoring rules, and the testing of results.
	Is less likely to be bound by arbitrary cut-off points.
Drawbacks	Can prove difficult to ensure consistency of assessment.
	Makes prioritisation and quick evaluation difficult.
	Will be more difficult to present, when seeking support and commitment.
	Is likely to be unwieldy and difficult to apply in large and complex organisations.
	Will be difficult to write into a procedure for the purposes of ISO14001.
Minimal qualitative assessment (Brainstorming)	This approach identifies, with the minimum of analysis, the most prominent environmental issues or pressures, identifies the related aspects and impacts, and takes these as significant. There may be some scoring to reduce the number of aspects or impacts if necessary.
	This can be suitable for ISO14001, if it is applied consistently and can be shown fully to cover the organisation's aspects and impacts (see case example). However, some certification bodies may be reluctant to accept this approach.
Benefits	Easy and quick to apply.
	Cost effective.
	Addresses commercial and environmental issues of direct importance to the business.
Drawbacks	Assessment is limited to existing understanding and knowledge.
	Commercial drivers are likely to dominate.
	Addressing the main issues and pressures may obscure some easier initial targets.
	It might not satisfy ISO14001 requirements.

Use of external criteria	This approach can be similar to the 'minimal qualitative approach', in that it establishes significance based upon criteria established by external parties. Commonly the criteria will be shaped by government, legislation, industry schemes and standards, voluntary codes, customers, or reporting conventions. This approach is unlikely to be suitable for ISO14001, unless this can be shown fully to cover the organisation's aspects and impacts.
Benefits	Easy and quick to apply Cost effective. Addresses the interests of key interested parties. Further information, guidance and support are likely to be available.
Drawbacks	It doesn't necessarily focus on the most significant aspects and impacts for your organisation. Some criteria might be difficult, complex and costly to address. It might not satisfy ISO14001 requirements.

Case example   Kennedy Construction Ltd: using the brainstorming approach and commercial criteria for impact significance assessment

Kennedy Construction covers water, gas electricity, telecoms and multi-utility civil engineering projects for a variety of utility and construction companies throughout the UK

Environmental aspects and related impacts were identified by a cross-functional team from within Kennedy.

From this process all the impacts identified were assessed for significance by considering where the greatest drivers for change existed (from within or outside the company) – i.e. risk, financial performance, marketing, views of interested parties or corporate values.

Where a driver was deemed to be very strong, the significance was coded red, moderate was coded amber and weak was coded green. Impacts where it was felt more information would be required were coded blue.

The colour coding allowed for a quick visual assessment of the overall significance of the impact. No numerical ranking was applied, instead any red code was seen as a priority for action, while amber would require careful monitoring and review. Green codes could not be ignored but would require a lower level of monitoring.

By assessing significance in this manner, Kennedy were able to focus environmental management efforts in areas where there were powerful commercial drivers. Also, the use of colour coding helped in the interpretation and communication of the information.

3.1.5.3   Assessing activities, products or services

If you have decided to conduct a more detailed and formal aspect and impact assessment (which will meet the requirements of ISO14001), then you will need, first, to identify the principal activities, products or services of your organisation for which you will identify related aspects and impacts. Some examples are detailed in Figure 22. Note that you can choose to look exclusively at activities, or products or services. Alternatively you can look at any mixture of the three if applicable. The danger of the latter approach is that you can find that there is some overlap between the three.

Figure 22   Examples of activities, products and services

Activity	• Production of pesticide H23
	• Vehicle washing
	• Maintenance of office equipment
	• Disposal of solid special wastes
	• Decommissioning of bulk storage silos.
Product	• Pesticide H23
	• Cardboard packaging
	• Light goods vans
	• 'Crunchers' children's novelty snack pack 25g, sports bag promotional pack
	• Scrap metal by-product (from decommissioning of bulk storage silos).
Service	• Pesticide packaging line cleaning
	• Contract distribution for 'Crunchers Snacks'
	• Pick and pack for mail order operation
	• Maintenance on leased office equipment
	• Demolition and scrap clearance of bulk storage silos.

In the majority of cases, the emphasis tends to be on activities, as these can be more generic and as such can reduce the amount of analysis required. Our examples in Figure 22 demonstrate this point for the 'Production of pesticide H23' and the 'Decommissioning of bulk storage silos'. Activities, however, do not tend to reach far beyond the bounds of the organisation, and may not always be suitable to look at in isolation.

Appendix 10 provides a template to assist you in the compilation of aspect and impact information by activity, product or service, as required. It might be worth using this template (or an electronic version) to record information as you progress through the steps of this stage.

3.1.5.4   Identifying environmental aspects

Once the activities, products or services which are to be assessed have been identified, you will then need to identify the environmental aspects specific to that facet of the organisation. Appendix 10 will help you compile the record of this assessment.

If you are struggling to identify aspects, then Appendix 9 (the brainstorming template) may provide some assistance. Remember, however, that this template lists environmental headings which could be either aspects or impacts, depending upon circumstances.

For example, the release of greenhouse gases as a result of burning fossil fuels would be classed as an impact (the burning of fossil fuels being the aspect). Whereas the use of greenhouse gases in refrigeration equipment would be classed as an aspect, one impact being any releases or leakage of the refrigeration gases to the atmosphere.

Figure 23 provides a fully completed example of Appendix 10 for reference, looking at fuel consumption through the use of company cars, and the provision of car parking facilities at head office.

Figure 23 **Example of completed aspect and impact significance assessment record (see Appendix 10)**

(1) Activity	Company Travel	
(2) Aspect	(3) Impact	(4) Significance
Fuel consumption through the use of company cars	• Non-renewable resource depletion	Moderate
	• Disruption to habitats and ecosystems through extraction and releases	Low
	• Emissions of	High
	○ CO_2 (contribute to global warming)	High
	○ CO (toxic to humans)	Moderate
	○ NO & NO_2 (contribute to acidification, human respiratory problems)	High
	○ VOCs (act as a catalyst for ground ozone creation with NO_2, and contain carcinogens)	High
	○ SO_2 (contribute to acidification and human respiratory problems)	High
	○ Particulate matter (cause human respiratory problems, and soiling).	Moderate
Provision of car parking facilities at head office	• Increased land requirement	Moderate
	• Leaching of fuel, lubricants and other chemicals (from vehicles) into ground, water bodies and drainage system	High
	• Light and noise pollution	Moderate
	• Reduction of local air quality due to emissions	Low
	• + Creation of nature reserves through the landscaping of parking area and reduction of visual intrusion	Moderate +

Note: Significance ratings are for demonstration purposes only. '+' Indicates a positive environmental impact.

Identifying environmental impacts

Once the aspects have been identified for the activities, products or services, it will then be necessary to identify the impacts on the environment arising.

Impacts which arise as a result of normal activity, such as land filling of solid waste generated from production lines, will generally be identifiable and predictable. However, you should also consider impacts on the environment which occur as a result of irregular, abnormal or emergency conditions.

For example, using the solid-waste scenario:

Condition	Impact
Normal	Solid waste from production lines land filled
Irregular	Special waste from cleaning process land filled
Abnormal	Faulty batch land filled
Emergency	Fumes emitted from stock as a result of fire in storage areas

Irregular impacts may well be identifiable and predictable, but abnormal and emergency situation related impacts will require the consideration of the probability of occurrence, and/or past records and experiences.

To ensure that the identification and assessment of impacts remain manageable, it may be necessary to conduct a rough appraisal of the significance of impacts as you go, with the aim of listing only the more significant impacts. While this may appear to undermine the next step, significance evaluation, some impacts are obviously going to prove insignificant, so it is only going to waste time and confuse matters by including them. In the event that you are uncertain about the significance of an impact, it is advisable to include it until such time as you can obtain more information.

As an example, two impacts from the operation of a modern office facility might be the related emissions to atmosphere from electricity consumption and the release of VOCs from the use of correction fluid. Both are environmental impacts, but the releases of VOCs from correction fluids are on such a small scale that they can be discounted even at this, the identification, stage.

Admittedly, not all situations will be so clear cut, which is why a more detailed approach to evaluating significance will be required.

Evaluating significance

In section 3.1.5.2, we defined significance and looked at some alternative approaches to its evaluation. From the identification of aspects and impacts which relate to a defined activity, product or service, it is now possible to evaluate significance, in order to enable identification and prioritisation of required actions and supporting indicators. The information collated through the stages of this section should also be taken into account when assessing the significance of an aspect or impact.

Significance evaluation can be performed at aspect or impact level. More commonly the aspect level is chosen, as this can be less involved and time consuming. However, this more generic level will make it more difficult to identify specific issues and actions, and can lead to less reliable results. Ultimately, you must weigh up the amount of work involved against the eventual benefit to be derived.

Remember, you are only trying to identify the most important aspects and/or impacts so that you can focus your activity under an EPE system and/or an EMS.

Appendix 10 provides space to record significance evaluations and also to make notes relating to each.

Some general guidelines are presented below which should be considered in any assessment of significance. These considerations, along with the different approaches to significance evaluation outlined in this step, will also influence the decision to evaluate aspects or impacts (or a mixture of the two).

- You will need to establish some rules for the assessment of significance which are clear and can be applied consistently.
- Consider the use of groups to evaluate significance, and/or peer review of results, to reduce the risk of missing or underestimating significance. Note that the more people involved in the process, the more precise your rules for evaluation will need to be. Furthermore, the process is likely to take longer, even if it is not much more time consuming (in terms of man hours).
- In deciding on the significance assessment process to apply, you should try to avoid processes which are overly complex, resource intensive and/or time consuming. Remember, the effort you commit to assessing significance needs to reflect the fact that significance evaluation is not an absolute science, and that ongoing reviews of results and processes will take place.

- Ongoing reviews of significance evaluation should form part of any management review process allowing for adjustments to be made if subsequently deemed necessary as a result of miscalculation or changes in circumstances.
- The development of explanatory notes and supporting evidence to accompany significance results can be useful in informing interested parties[2] and avoiding misperceptions of the impact your organisation has on the environment. Providing this sort of supporting data can also assist in convincing interested parties of the importance of environmental action and in securing commitment.
- To obtain a better understanding of the significance of an impact, measures of activity, or details of products or services, could be required. This information may well be most useful in the form of an indicator, or indeed form the basis for indicators developed later on in the EPE system development.
- Where sufficient influence can be exerted to make positive changes, organisations can consider impacts which occur beyond the bounds of their own facilities or activities. Where such indirect impacts exist, commercial pressures may well dictate that organisations have a responsibility to exert an influence. The assessment of impacts outside direct control is often far more difficult and resource intensive than for the internal.
- Appraisal of the frequency, severity, scale and duration of any impact occurrences can be taken into account when determining significance for normal and predictable situations. Abnormal and emergency situations, on the other hand, will require as well an assessment and consideration of the probability of the impact occurring.

When rating significance, you can apply numerical scores, or use colours, symbols, letters or any other defining marks to identify a significance rating.

Numerical approaches are the most commonly applied, as these present opportunities for creating more levels of significance, and also for the manipulation and consolidation of scores throughout the significance assessment process. This flexibility, however, can also present a number of pitfalls, in that it encourages the creation of complex and unwieldy systems which are difficult to use, difficult to explain and often produce unreliable information with subjectivity built in at many levels.

If you choose to use a scoring system:

- Keep the range of scores to a minimum (e.g. 1 = low significance to 3 = high significance), this will assist consistent application, and recognises the fact that most significance evaluation is so subjective that achieving any greater accuracy is unrealistic.

[2] Note, that ISO14031 and ISO14001 do not stipulate a requirement to report environmental information externally.

- Resist excessive manipulation and consolidation of scores, as this will only serve to make the final results less relevant or understandable, unless very strong supporting documentation has been developed as well.
- Maintain a focus on the real nature of the aspect or impact that you are evaluating, as scoring systems can often create distortions, and there will always be a tendency to create arbitrary cut-off points when deciding on which aspects or impacts to tackle.

Systems which employ colours, or symbols of some sort, are inevitably less flexible, but certainly in less complex situations this lack of flexibility can assist the user by making consistent application easier to control, and by removing the temptation to concentrate on numbers rather than real issues. Such systems can also be so presented as to have a greater visual impact than numerical systems. The case example on p.85 applied a 'traffic light' colour-scoring method. Here the most significant aspects were coded red and stood out clearly from all the other aspects. Obviously, good presentation can achieve similar results for numerical systems, but where numbers exist there is often a tendency to focus on values.

Whatever evaluation approach you adopt, Figure 24 provides a flow chart which you can follow to try and ensure that reliable results are obtained, that necessary supporting notes are created and that feedback is sought and received.

Throughout this section and 3.1.5.2 we have mentioned the problems which can be created by subjective evaluation of significance. Some degree of subjectivity is inevitable, even where detailed rules have been devised and group or peer review is employed, and you should be aware that significance evaluations will not always be reliable and can change over time as perceptions alter and more information and understanding are gained.

3.1.5.7 Summarising significance assessments and prioritising aspects and impacts

With Appendix 10 now completed for each of the activities, products or services identified, it will be useful to prioritise the aspects and/or impacts by level of significance. Consolidating the information for the most significant aspects and/or impacts across all activities, products and services reviewed will provide you with an overview of the key aspects and impacts to address under the EPE system, and possibly any EMS activity as well.

Figure 24   Process for improving the reliability of significance evaluation outputs

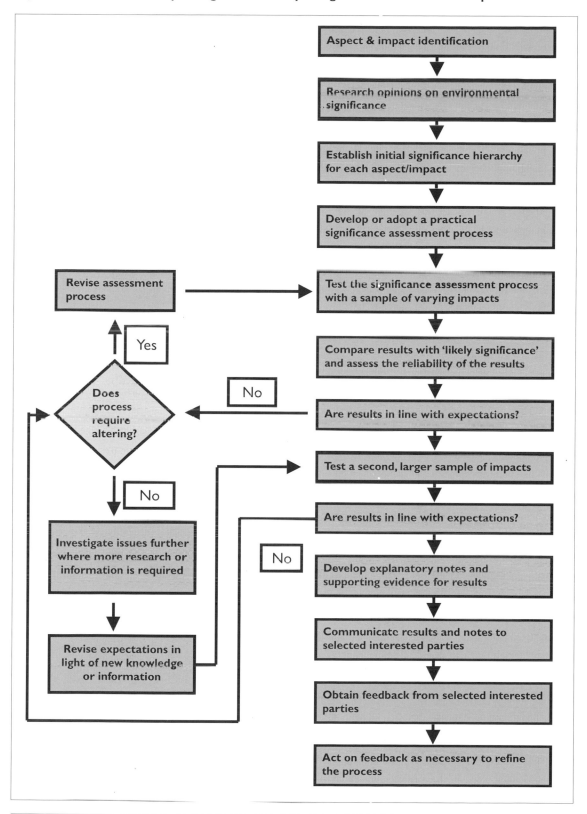

Clear presentation of this summary will provide useful supporting information when attempting to raise awareness and understanding, and secure commitment.

Section 3.1 checklist

Before you embark on the next stages of EPE implementation you should have:

○ Prepared a summary of all the relevant legislative and voluntary requirements, developments, exposure and opportunities

○ Prepared a summary prioritising existing and proposed environmental performance criteria, with supporting information

○ Prepared a summary of the principal views, issues and expectations of interested parties

○ Prepared a prioritised summary of costs and benefits

○ Prepared a prioritised summary of significant environmental aspects and impacts

---

Task Heading	**Features of your organisation**
Section Reference	**3.2**
Duration	3 man days +
Difficulty Rating	3
Aims & Objectives	The aim of this section is to identify the key features of your organisation which will have an influence on the design, implementation and operation of the EPE system. By following each stage in this section you will be able to list the key influences for the organisation which need accommodating or addressing in the development of plans.
Outputs	The principal outputs of this section will be: • The examination of existing practices and procedures • The assessment of the structure of your organisation • The asessment of the culture of your organisation • The identification of potential barriers and opportunities.
Resources Considerations People	Project manager Core EPE team Top management Functional management Operational management Supervisory staff Advisers or consultants
Physical	Work station and office facilities Meeting facilities Access to information Honesty
Outputs from Previous Tasks	An outline plan with timescales and milestones for developing an EPE system. Section 2.3.2 An outline of initial resource requirements to achieve the first milestone. Section 2.3.3 Initial top management commitment. Section 2.3.4
Potential Problems	• Lack of organisational understanding • Lack of honesty or objective self-assessment within the organisation • Lack of necessary resources • Limited range of input or consultation • Over-analytical approach to structure and culture of the organisation • High level of subjective assumption and emotive reaction.
Potential Opportunities	• Identification of restrictions that need accommodating or addressing • Identification of existing features that can assist EPE development. • Greater understanding of internal interested parties' aspirations and expectations.

3.2.1 Examining existing practices and procedures

> The principal outputs of this stage will be:
>
> O   The identification of existing practices and procedures which are currently providing environmental information
>
> O   The identification of other practices and procedures in existence which could be utilised or will influence new system design
>
> O   A summary of the examination findings

Unlike the examination of existing practices and procedures undertaken when establishing an EMS, which focus on the ability to control or improve, the requirements for EPE development will centre upon the ability to provide relevant and reliable information or data.

If your organisation currently operates a formal EMS, it is likely that there will be a range of practices and procedures in operation which currently provide information or will have an influence on the way any EPE system is developed. In such cases the examination of existing practices and procedures will be facilitated, but it is important not to ignore other processes and practices within the organisation which present opportunities or constraints for the development of the EPE system.

If a formal EMS is not in place, then greater emphasis will probably have to be placed on looking at the practices and processes of various areas of the business.

3.2.1.1 Identifying existing practices and procedures which are currently providing environmental information

From the identification of key issues, pressures, aspects and impacts (in section 3.1), you should focus on identifying any practices and/or procedures which are currently in operation that provide information about these areas.

Appendix 11, provides a template for recording the findings of this examination. First you will need to identify each practice or procedure and the issue, pressure aspect or impact which it relates most closely to. For example, taking water-meter readings weekly (as the practice) and water usage (as the aspect).

Having identified the key practices and procedures, you will then need to assess the data provided by each. Appendix 11 identifies the principal considerations as column headings, providing space for information to be entered. In addition to this, however, some further considerations are identified in Figure 25, which can be used as a checklist, and further information can be added into new spare columns.

The far right hand columns have been reserved for you to rank the reliability and relevance of the data provided, should you so require. This might prove useful when developing the EPE system, by identifying which data streams you want to continue using and which need improving.

Figure 25 **Further considerations when examining existing practices and procedures**

• How is data collected? • How is data communicated? • Who is the data communicated to? • What terms of expression are used? • Are current terms of expression clearly understood by users and recipients of data? • How much conversion of data is applied and how well is this understood? • Where is the data held? • How easily can the practice or procedure be adapted?	• How accessible is the data? • Are there any official restrictions on circulation of the data? • How easily can the data be handled (i.e. transferred, and manipulated)? • At what level is the data collected and held (i.e. to what extent has data been aggregated and can it be broken down to its simplest form)? • Is historical data compatible, reliable, manageable or relevant? • Are there any reasons why the practice or procedure must be incorporated into any future EPE?

3.2.1.2 Identifying other practices and procedures in existence which could be utilised or will influence new system design

This section differs from 3.2.1.1 insofar as it will look at practices and procedures applied within the organisation for data and information provision that are not specifically designed to support the management of environmental issues, pressures, aspects or impacts.

If we take our example from section 3.2.1.1, it is likely that water-consumption information will exist on invoices issued to your organisation, and this will reside with the accounts department. Chances are that the accounts department do not look at the quantity of water used, or when and where it is used. Their prime consideration will be how much the invoice is for, and some tolerance parameters will probably exist to trigger further investigation if the invoice total is outside these.

In identifying practices and procedures which could be utilised, Appendix 11 can be used again, only this time you will be best advised to identify the key issues, pressures, aspects and impacts first and then look for practices and procedures which might help.

When considering practices and procedures which might influence the design of any EPE system, the information can also be recorded using Appendix 11, but in this case you will need to identify practices and procedures which are central to the organisation, and any information management and reporting systems. An example of this might be where a standard method of communicating information through the organisation is stipulated.

3.2.1.3 Summarising the examination findings

Summarising the examination outputs will help you identify the most important practices and procedures currently operating within the organisation, and also identify where improvements are required. This information will also allow you quickly to assess what data-generating practices and procedures will be required when you establish indicators in section 3.5.

3.2.2 Assessing organisational structure and culture

The principal outputs from this stage wil be:

O   The assessment of key variables in organisational structure

O   The assessment of key variables in organisational culture

3.2.2.1 Organisational structure

The structure of your organisation is likely to have a major influence on the design of an effective EPE system. You will probably know and understand the organisational structure within which you operate, and obtaining any additional information is likely to be relatively straightforward.

Appendix 12 provides a template for the assessment and summarisation of your organisational structure. Principal variables in organisational structure are provided as prompts in the left-hand column, but there is also space to add in any others that are relevant. The next column provides space to record the structural details of your organisation, and the next column provides space to note any likely impacts that the structure will have on EPE development.

Figure 26 identifies for your reference some of the likely impacts that organisational-structure variables can have on EPE development.

3.2.2.2 Organisational culture

Unlike organisational structure, understanding of organisational culture is likely to be more subjective, given that you are likely to be so close to it and will have built up certain perceptions. Using input from other parties, as appropriate, to test your beliefs, may well help you conduct a more objective assessment.

Figure 26 **Likely impacts of organisational structure on EPE development**

Variables In Organisational Structure	Likely Impacts on EPE Development
Product or service orientated	Product-orientated organisations are likely to find that the EPE system will focus heavily on OPIs, whereas service-orientated organisations may have to rely more heavily on MPIs. Product orientation will also tend to require more consideration of the supply chain, though the products used by service providers may also require attention.
Number of sites or operating locations, subdivisions or functions	The greater the number and spread of operating sites, subdivisions or functions, the larger the task will be to implement a consistent and integrated EPE system. In view of this, it might be favourable for sites, divisions or functions to develop EPE autonomously or as regional, divisional or activity based groups.
Range of activities and technologies	A wide range of activities or technologies will make it more difficult to apply an EPE system uniformly across the organisation. Similarly, the relevance of data, collection methods and data quality are likely to vary greatly. This is of particular importance if performance is to be compared between units.
Labour or capital intensive	The measurement of environmental data is likely to be more manually orientated in labour-intensive operations than in capital-intensive ones. Manual data collation will mean a greater requirement for training, verification and checking, while mechanical measurement systems will require calibration checks. However, greater flexibility in data collation and reporting will be possible with manual systems.
Stability of workforce	A workforce with a high turnover rate is likely to cause problems with the reliability of the data collected and/or training provision for data collection, if data collection responsibility sits with this workforce. Some cultural issues may be assisted by high turnover and instability, while other will be exacerbated. The motivational value of EPE systems may also be weakened when staff turnover is high.
Clarity of responsibilities and nature of reporting lines	Clearly defined responsibilities will make investigation, planning, implementation and operation of an EPE system much easier. It will also help in getting people to take ownership of issues, objectives and targets. This in turn will help in identifying internal interested parties and the sort of information and terminology required of the EPE system.
Nature of reporting structure and communication lines	The nature of reporting lines will influence the design of data-communication systems. In addition it will affect the volume and complexity of the data that can be handled, and the speed with which they are communicated.

Variables in Organisational Structure	Likely Impacts on EPE Development
Flexibility for change	Flexible organisational structures, while potentially advantageous from a cultural perspective when introducing an EPE system or enacting change, may well create difficulties when trying to operate a meaningful set of indicators. Rapid change could require constant review and alterations to the system and invalidate historical data. On the other hand, frequent change may provide opportunities to act on performance data to make improvements at each change.
Formal or informal management structures	Formal structures are likely to provide more support to any EPE system than informal structures, though other structural factors will probably have more influence on the overall effectiveness of the EPE.
Centralised or decentralised	From a whole-organisation perspective, centralised structures would appear to offer more scope for developing a sophisticated and cohesive EPE system than decentralised ones. However, as touched on already, decentralised organisations may be able to develop more-relevant and more-effective EPE systems within their operating units than relying on a central function.

In a similar style to the section on organisational structure, this section will concentrate on looking at some common cultural variables and the potential impact that these can have on the development of an EPE system.

Appendix 13, provides a template for the assessment and summarisation of your organisational culture, and will work along the lines of the template in Appendix 12. Figure 27, also provides some likely impacts associated with different variables of organisational culture which might assist your assessment.

Recognising cultural restrictions during the planning stage will, firstly, enable you to develop an EPE system which complements the current culture, and secondly identify areas where cultural change is desirable. From this it will be possible to plan activities that will facilitate any changes over time, and establish measures to track these.

Figure 27 **Likely impacts of organisation culture on EPE development**

Variables in Organisational Culture	Likely Impacts on EPE Development
Management focus, i.e. sales, production, marketing	The management focus of the organisation will shape any environmental criteria and consequently influence the focus of indicators in the EPE system. A marketing focussed organisation will seek indication of the environmental qualities of a product or new product developments, where as production led organisations may focus more on operational factors.

Variables in Organisational Culture	Likely Impacts on EPE Development
Proactive or reactive	Proactive organisations will probably look for information on trends and progress where as reactive organisations may be more interested in policing measures which track compliance with criteria retrospectively. Reactive organisations may be less inclined to develop the EPE system continuously (if at all) than proactive ones.
Open or reserved	Selecting the most suitable indicators, gaining commitment, obtaining reliable data, and using EPE as a motivational tool, will all be helped in an open and honest culture, but hindered in a reserved and suspicious one.
Importance of traditions and history	The traditions and history of an organisation can facilitate the development of an EPE, for example if the organisation has traditionally been at the forefront of management excellence.
Level of autonomy or empowerment	The level of empowerment through the organisation will dictate how wide-reaching the EPE system can be. Autonomy can present opportunities and problems depending on how you want the system to operate.
Relationships between management and staff	Relationships between management and staff can potentially affect data quality, the ability to drive improvements, and the ability to get to the root cause of performance issues.
Relationships between managers	Relationships between managers will also be an important factor in the consistent operation of the EPE and the commitment to making it work and using it to drive improvement. In competitive situations EPE can be very emotive, championed by some, rubbished by others, however, if the system is regarded as fair, then far greater improvements can be achieved more quickly in this culture.
Extent to which people are target orientated and have commitment to achieving agreed levels of performance	EPE systems are likely to be much easier to implement in organisations where targeting and measurement are widely applied. However, the impact of an EPE system is likely to far greater in an organisation unused to such approaches, and as such might raise the profile of environmental management above other areas.
Attitudes towards innovation	Reluctance to embrace innovative approaches and ideas may well hinder the development and adoption of an EPE system, especially where it is perceived as a threat to the status quo.
Attitudes towards costs	Highly cost conscious management will be keen to track the financial aspects of environmental performance, for which indicators can be developed. Longer term, this may hold the EPE development back if early savings are not continued. Less cost conscious management might allow for the development of a more balanced EPE approach.
Attitudes towards investment	The development and implementation of an EPE system will require resources before it can demonstrate benefits. The focus of the EPE may need to be geared to measuring tangible benefits in a short-term investment culture.

Variables in Organisational Culture	Likely Impacts on EPE Development
Level of commitment and loyalty of staff to the organisation	The availability, and reliability of data, and the ability to drive improvements through an EPE system, will be influenced by the commitment, and loyalty of staff. It may be possible to develop indicators, which reflect the commitment of different individuals or groups, and as such allow management of these issues more effectively.
Elitism or tolerant development	The nature of the EPE system needs to acknowledge how it is likely to be used to motivate people to make improvements. Elitist cultures will probably seek to use EPE to identify and reward the best performers while targeting the worst for remedial action. Here equity needs to run though the system, whereas this is less important where EPE is used to identify development needs.
Attitudes towards risk	Whether an organisation's management are risk tolerant or risk averse, will shape any environmental criteria and consequently influence the focus of indicators in the EPE system.

3.2.3 Potential barriers and opportunities

The principal outputs from this section will be

○ The identification of potential barriers to the successful implementation of an EPE system

○ The identification of potential opportunities relating to the implementation of an EPE system

○ The prioritisation and summary of potential barriers and opportunities

From the assessment work carried out so far, it should be possible to identify some barriers to the development and implementation of an EPE system, as well as identifying opportunities.

It will be useful to compile a prioritised summary of all the main barriers and opportunities identified at this stage of the process, which can then be fed into the development process at later stages. Where barriers exist which will require immediate attention, plans to address these should be prepared, approved and then actioned before further work is undertaken.

Figure 28 provides an example of some potential barriers and opportunities, and how they can be summarised.

Figure 28 Example of a 'barriers and opportunities' summary

Potential Barriers	Rating	Potential Opportunities	Rating
Securing commitment from operational managers	5	Saving in operations through tighter resource and waste management	4
Lack of personal computers to enable collection and reporting of data	4	Ability to track and manage performance against legislation	3
High turnover of operational staff	2	Opportunity to provide major customers with information on environmental performance	3
Large number of sites with wide range of activities, products and services	2	Potential to build an ISO14001 environmental management system, supported by EPE information	1

Rating: 1 = lowest importance, 5 = highest importance

Note: ratings are provided only for demonstrative purposes, as actual rankings will be dependent upon the specific circumstances of your organisation.

Section 3.2 checklist

Before you embark on the next stages of EPE implementation you should have:

O Prepared a summary of existing practices and procedures within the organisation

O Assessed the key variables in organisational structure

O Assessed the key variables in organisational culture

O Prepared a prioritised summary of potential barriers and opportunities facing the implementation of an EPE system within your organisation

---

Task Heading	**Developing clear direction and goals**
Section Reference	**3.3**
Duration	1 man day +
Difficulty Rating	3

Aims & Objectives	The aim of this section is to define clearly a direction and goals for the EPE project, building on the initial vision developed (see section 2.3.1), and using the outputs from sections 3.1 and 3.2. You will also develop a clear understanding of the relative importance of issues, pressures and organisational features, in relation to the development of an EPE system and environmental management. By following each stage in this section you will develop a clearly stated direction and goals, which will provide the focus for developing, implementing and operating the EPE system.
Outputs	The principal outputs of this section will be: • The assessment and analysis of the outputs from sections 3.1 and 3.2 • The development of a direction and goals for the EPE system, which are appropriate to the organisation • A refined vision of what the EPE system will deliver for the organisation • A revised outline of resource requirements, and timescales for achieving milestones • A schedule for presenting to or communicating with the most important management representatives and groups, i.e. those whose commitment is required, and the arrangement of facilities and necessary support • Presentation and support material to facilitate securing management commitment (tailored to needs) based on the outputs of this section.
Resources Considerations People	Project manager Core EPE team Top management Advisers or consultants
Physical	Work station and office facilities Meeting facilities Vision, honesty and realism Access to analysis tools Access to presentation materials and/or media
Outputs from Previous Tasks	Information on issues and pressures. Section 3.1 Information on influencing features. Section 3.2
Potential Problems	• Large and wide-ranging set of information to consider • Insufficient investigation or analysis at earlier stages • Sensitivity of issues, pressures and/or features within the organisation • Lack of consensus within core EPE team and/or key management groups • Lack of analytical and presentation competencies

Potential Opportunities	• Motivation of core EPE team and key interested parties through the provision of a clear focus to the EPE activity
	• Getting an early buy-in to the project from key interested parties through involvement at this stage
	• Building relationships
	• Utilising existing features of the organisation to advance the development of the EPE system.

Developing a clear direction and goals for the EPE system is of utmost importance in order to facilitate the securing of management commitment, and to maintain the focus of the system on the most important environmental issues and areas.

The work carried out under sections 3.1 and 3.2 will have provided background information, which should form the basis of any direction and goals developed.

3.3.1 Assessment and analysis of outputs

The principal outputs from this stage will be:

○ The development of a matrix to help you assess the current position of the organisation in relation to environmental aspects, impacts, issues and pressures

○ The appraisal of key features of the organisation

3.3.1.1 Developing a matrix to assess environmental position

An important part of defining direction and goals in any project is understanding where you are now. This step of the stage aims to allow a clear picture to be developed through the use of a matrix, which will be developed through the rest of this section.

If your organisation already operates a formal EMS, it is likely that you will have a direction and goals already defined, possibly stated as an 'environmental policy', with objectives and targets. In this event it is going to be more suitable to use this EMS-based framework as the foundation for the determining of a direction and goals. However, the techniques described in this stage, and beyond, may well help you highlight additional areas upon which you would want to focus the EPE system.

Appendix 14 provides a template which can be used for the creation of a matrix. The matrix will require you to draw on information and knowledge gathered in section 3.1.

The matrix (as shown in Appendix 14) requires that you identify a primary focus from:

- Significant aspects and/or impacts
- Legislation and regulation
- Organisational environmental performance criteria
- The views of interested parties
- Costs and benefits.

Of the headings above, those which you have not selected as your primary focus will become secondary considerations.

The direction of the EPE system will be determined by the primary focus, so it is important to consider carefully what it is you want to achieve with the eventual EPE system. In keeping with the intent of ISO14031, it is suggested that you select significant environmental aspects and/or impacts as the primary focus, as this is most likely to drive improvements across a range of environmental impacts. However, cultural pressures in the organisation may force you to focus more heavily on legislation or costs, for example.

Whichever primary focus is selected, it is important to consider any important factors which might have been overlooked as a result, and to include these as appropriate (the matrix provides for this).

Figure 29, gives an example of how the matrix should be completed, at this step, taking significant aspects as the primary focus.

Figure 29 Example of matrix completion for stage 3.3.1.1

Primary Focus **Significant Aspects**	Secondary Considerations	Category
Electricity use	Indirect CO_2 Emissions Climate change levy Cost of electricity	L/V C/B C/B
Water consumption and discharge	Terms of discharge consent Cost of drawing water from mains Cost of treating water prior to discharge Cost of discharge consent	L/V C/B C/B C/B
Packaging	Producer responsibility regulations Packaging minimisation regulations (essential requirements) Passing on costs to customers related to disposal, recycling and regulatory requirements Cost of materials	L/V L/V IP C/B

Primary Focus **Significant Aspects**	Secondary Considerations	Category
Packaging continued	Use of PVC in packaging	IP
	Use of a minimum of 97% recycled material in outer packaging	PC
Solid-waste generation	Legislation governing duty of care requirements for disposal, recycling and recovery	L/V
	Landfill rates and taxes	C/B
	Waste carriage charges	C/B
	Waste handling and storage on site	IP
	Increased consumption of materials related to increased waste proportions	C/B

Key to category abbreviations:

A/I = Aspect or impact

L/V = Legal or voluntary requirement

PC = Organisational performance criteria

IP = View of interested party or parties

C/B = Cost or benefit

Once all significant aspects and impacts have been addressed in the matrix, it is possible that there are factors which have not been considered as they do not relate directly to any significant aspect or impact. Examples could be:

- The certification of the EMS to ISO14001 (as a performance criteria)
- The production of a corporate environmental report (to meet the requirements of interested parties)
- The provision of recycling bins for drinks cups and cans (as an insignificant aspect which presents motivational opportunities and/or revenue generation at little or no cost).

3.3.1.2 The appraisal of key features of the organisation

It is important that you have, as part of understanding the current situation, a clear view of the critical features of the organisation which may influence the development, implementation and operation of the EPE system. The prioritised summaries created in section 3.2 should provide the basis for this, if not a concise summary in themselves.

3.3.2 Developing direction and goals

> The principal output from this stage will be:
>
> O   Identification of what you want to achieve against each entry in the matrix
>
> O   Assessment of the principal barriers which potentially hinder achievement
>
> O   Assessment of the opportunities presented to facilitate achievement
>
> O   An outline view of how the goals identified wil be achieved.

3.3.2.1 Identifying achievement aspirations

Having completed the first steps in the matrix (see Appendix 14), the next step is to identify what you want to achieve against each entry. At this stage, these achievement aspirations need not be highly detailed, and indeed while detail will be useful at later stages it is possible that it will overcomplicate the matrix for assessment purposes.

Figure 30 provides some examples of achievement aspirations or expectations in the context of packaging from the examples shown in Figure 29.

Figure 30   **Example aspirations and expectations for environmental performance**

Significant Aspect	Secondary Considerations	Aspirations and Expectations
Packaging	Producer responsibility regulations	Ensure compliance with legislation at least cost
	Packaging minimisation regulations (essential requirements)	Ensure compliance with legislation at least cost
	Passing on costs to customers related to disposal, recycling and regulatory requirements	Redesign and reduce packaging to minimise the costs incurred by customers
	Cost of materials	Redesign and reduce packaging consumption and waste
	Use of PVC in packaging	Gauge customer and consumer attitudes to PVC packaging and potential alternatives to support further action
	Use of a minimum of 97% recycled material in outer packaging	Ensure that outer packaging contains a minimum of 97% recycled material

3.3.2.2 Assessment of barriers to achievement

Having identified the aspirations and expectations for each entry, it is important to identify where barriers exist to achieving these goals. The work carried out in stage 3.2.3 and the summary developed in 3.3.1.2 should provide you with most of this information, though it is possible that further barriers will become apparent when you start to assess specific goals.

Significant barriers identified should be entered into Appendix 14, alongside the aspirations and expectations column.

3.3.2.3 Assessment of opportunities presented

In similar fashion to barriers, it is useful to identify any opportunities which may facilitate the realisation of the stated goals.

3.3.2.4 Outlining plans for achieving stated goals

The final step in this stage is to outline plans for achieving the goals stated in Appendix 14. These plans will need to consider the barriers and opportunities identified, and it is possible that some plans will be capable of covering more than one goal.

In view of this Appendix 15 provides a separate template for the summarisation of goals and outline plans.

The plans developed will form the focus of environmental management activity within the organisation, and consequently the focus of the EPE system. While activity to address the goals established will be additional to the activity required for the establishment of the EPE system, the two will be closely related. If there is an understanding of what the goals are but no idea of how they will be achieved, then the development of an effective and appropriate EPE system will be very difficult.

As an example, if you have a stated goal to ensure legal compliance with packaging legislation, yet you do not have any plan as to how you will achieve this, it will be difficult to establish indicators which can measure how well the organisation is performing, other than by the occurrence of legislative breaches. In many cases this will be too late.

In addition to this, on a more practical note, if you don't have any plans for making improvements, it is unlikely that aspirations will be recognised. Given this, the measurement of performance becomes devalued as a management exercise, and many of the potential benefits will not be realised.

3.3.3 Refining the vision of what you want to achieve

> The principal output of this stage will be:
>
> O   The review and amendment of the original EPE project vision in light of work subsequently undertaken as part of the planning phase

The original vision developed of what the implementation and operation of an EPE system would deliver for the organisation (section 2.3.1.5) may well need revisiting in light of investigative work and the development of direction, goals and activity plans to address environmental issues, pressures, aspect and impacts.

The purpose of refining the vision statement at this stage is to allow you to bring it into line with the direction and goals developed for environmental activity as a whole. Recognition and realisation of barriers and opportunities can also influence the nature of the vision, which will form the basis for further EPE activity.

3.3.4 Reviewing resource requirements and timescales

> The principal output from this stage will be:
>
> O   The revision and amendment, as appropriate, of outline predicitons of timescales and resource requirements, for the development of an EPE system

It is worthwhile reviewing the outline plan agreed when securing initial top management commitment, and making adjustments to some of the predictions made, in light of the work carried out to date.

Identification of issues and pressures, assessment of features of the organisation, and recognition of barriers and opportunities can all enable more-accurate predictions to be made over resource and time requirements. In addition to this, changes may have occurred since the original plan was agreed which will affect some of the assumptions upon which the plan was developed.

Further to this, it will be important to consider the effect that environmental activity plans will have on the development of the EPE system. For example, the training of staff in waste handling and storage techniques may be required before training on the measurement of waste can be delivered effectively. Conversely, time and resources may be freed up by other environmental activity.

The planning charts utilised in the initial planing phases (see stages 2.3.2 and 2.3.3 and Appendices 2 and 3) can be utilised to assist in this review.

3.3.5 Scheduling and preparing presentations and communications

> The principal outputs from this stage will be:
>
> ○ The identification of the management representatives and groups whose commitment will be required
>
> ○ The development of a schedule to present to the management parties identified
>
> ○ The preparation of presentations and communications which will support the securing of management commitment at the necessary levels

Securing further management commitment at this stage is suggested, as the selection of indicators (to be covered in section 3.5) is best carried out with the understanding, commitment and involvement of parties across relevant sectors of the business.

The size and structure of the organisation, coupled with the extent of commitment gained in the initial stages, may well remove the need to gain further commitment at this stage, and thus you will need to decide now whether you need to go through this stage and the following section 3.4.

3.3.5.1 Identifying key management representatives and groups

As part of output of identifying key interested parties (section 3.1.3), the most important management groups and individuals within the organisation should have been identified. This will assist you in identifying those management representatives and groups from whom you will need to secure commitment for the continuation of the EPE project. It is important to note that, even when top management commitment has been secured for the entire project at an early stage, it will probably be necessary to gain the support of managers at a lower level as well, if the project is to be successful.

Figure 31 identifies some management areas beyond the senior management team where it might be necessary to gain commitment to the project. Not all of these areas will necessarily be important, depending upon the extent and scope of the envisaged EPE system and the preparatory work done.

Figure 31 **Examples of potential key management areas to secure commitment with**

Finance and accounts	Research and development
Site or regional managers	Customer and after sales service
Purchasing	Product design and specification
Operations	IT and communications
Engineering	Forecasting
Logistics	Human resources or personnel
Fleet control	Administration
Facilities or site services	Special projects
Quality assurance	Health and safety
Sales, account and contract managers	Public relations
Marketing	Third-party contract managers

(This list is not in any order of priority)

In identifying key parties, it is often advisable to involve more parties, at the risk of including unimportant parties, rather than omitting any important parties, since securing commitment from these parties retrospectively will be even more difficult.

3.3.5.2 Developing a presentation schedule

From the identification of the key management representatives and groups whom you will need to present to and communicate with to secure commitment, it will next be necessary to schedule the presentations and communications.

The timing of this scheduling, ahead of delivery, will be determined by the availability of the key parties, suitable facilities, equipment and materials. In addition, consideration will need to be given to the period over which presentations and communications will take place, as it may well be impractical to deliver to all parties at once, or that different levels of presentation are planned for different parties.

Some tips on scheduling presentations are provided below.

* Establish when facilities, equipment, materials, support staff and specialist input are available
* Try to reach as many of the identified parties as possible
* Preserve flexibility in your schedule to accommodate parties who may have been overlooked when drawing up initial lists
* Schedule presentations and communications close together to maintain momentum, and to avoid alienating later parties
* If different presentations and communications are required at different levels of the organisation, ensure that these are scheduled to occur in the correct sequence – note that some slack might have to be built in to accommodate any slippage with the earlier approaches

- Schedule presentations and communications to accommodate the needs of the audience, this reduces the potential for animosity, and excuses
- Make the schedule achievable for the presenters or communication media
- Give people plenty of notice and avoid frequent alterations
- Ensure key senior managers will attend, and inform other parties of the fact – this can raise the profile of the event and encourage attendance
- Allow sufficient time in the schedule to accommodate feedback from the parties involved – this is of particular importance where feedback is required for the next level of presentations or communications.

The scheduling of presentations and communications should highlight any issues with planned timescales. It may be necessary to review the overall project plan timescales, if estimates for securing top management commitment were optimistic, or where scheduling problems have arisen.

3.3.5.3 Preparing presentations and communications

In attempting to secure management commitment for the EPE project, you will need to address the following areas.

- Some background to EPE and ISO14031
- The vision of what you expect to achieve through the implementation of an ISO14031 EPE system
- The key issues, pressures, aspects and impacts which relate to the organisation
- Outline plans of action to address these issues, pressures, aspects and impacts
- The plan of how you will implement and operate the EPE system
- An invitation, or request, for contributions to the programme from the audience – this might include pre-planned action points for attendees to sign up to at the meeting
- Opportunity for questions, discussion, debate, feedback and the provision of further information.

Under each of the above points it will be important to try to identify specific points of the project which will generate enthusiasm or interest among the audience. For example, opportunity for cost savings, increased sales, assistance with managing a difficult area or support for achieving established objectives and targets. If audiences vary greatly, it might be necessary to tailor the message accordingly. However, you should ensure that a consistent message and understanding are maintained.

Presenting information in a clear and concise format will undoubtedly assist in the process, but also think about innovative ways of presenting the information to add impact to specific points or issues.

For personal presentations, the provision of information beforehand may help to inform attendees, and allow them to contribute more constructively during the presentation. This pre-communication can often take the heat out of contentious issues, by providing the opportunity to present some information and detail up-front. Alternatively it can bring issues out into the open early on, preventing their being ignored or brushed over.

Depending upon the existing level of awareness of environmental management and business-related issues, EPE and international standards, it might well be necessary to provide some background and contextual information as part of the proposal. Background and contextual information is particularly suited to pre-communications, but providing excessive amounts of information can switch attendees off and/or detract from the impact of your message.

Finally, remember that the aim of the proposal is to secure commitment to progress with the project-planning phase. The final commitment to implement the EPE system will need to be secured once the planning phase has been completed. Commitment secured at this stage will facilitate the development of adequate plans for implementation and operation, and also initiate relationship and project-profile building. Seek to secure commitment (or to establish a date by which to receive a decision) at the time of these presentations and communications, if possible, in order to maintain the momentum.

(Some further tips on preparing presentations and communications can be found in section 2.3.3.)

Section 3.3 checklist

Before you embark on the next stages of EPE implementation you should have:

- O Developed a matrix to help you assess the current position of the organisation in relation to environmental aspects, impacts, issues and pressures

- O Conducted an appraisal of key features of the organisation

- O Created an outline view of how the goals identified will be achieved

- O Reviewed and amended the original EPE project vision

- O Revised and amended as appropriate, the outline predictions of timescales and resource requirements for the development of an EPE system

- O Identified the management representatives and groups whose commitment will be required

- O Developed a schedule to present to the management parties identified

- O Prepared presentations and communications which will support the securing of management commitment at the necessary levels.

Task Heading	**Gaining agreement and further management commitment**
Section Reference	**3.4**
Duration	1 man day +
Difficulty Rating	4
Aims & Objectives	The aim of this section is to provide guidance on how to secure real management commitment from all key management representatives and groups as identified in section 3.3.

By following the stages of this section it is intended that you will have secured real management commitment, or identified requirements for further activity. |
| Outputs | The principal outputs of this section will be:
• Presentation to, and/or communication with, key management representatives and groups
• Feedback from key management representatives and groups
• Evaluation of the level of commitment secured
• A plan of required activity to ensure that real commitment is secured (if required)
• Identification of additional barriers to EPE system development
• Revision of plans (if necessary)
• Agreed outline of resource requirements, timescales and milestones
• Acknowledgement of commitment secured
• A plan of activity to utilise commitment and reward providers
• List of commitments made and/or conditions agreed |
| Resources Considerations | |
| People | Project manager
Core EPE team
Top management
Key management representatives
Advisers or consultants |
| Physical | Work station and office facilities
Meeting facilities
Access to presentation and/or communications equipment and media
Transport |
| Outputs from Previous Tasks | The schedule for presenting or communicating. Section 3.3.5
Presentation and support material. Section 3.3.5.3
The vision of what the EPE system will deliver for the organisation. Section 3.3.3
The revised outline of resource requirements and timescales. Section 3.3.4 |
| Potential Problems | • Lack of presentation competencies
• Hidden agendas and political infighting
• Inconsistency of message
• Weak or unclear presentation or communication
• Timings of presentations or communications indicate perceived importance of key players in project
• Timings of presentations or communications allow for audience to receive message through other channels. |

Potential Opportunities	• Establish the value of the project in contributing to overall organisational aims
	• Gain strong commitment and buy-in from key players
	• Build relationships with key players
	• Establish credibility for the project and team
	• Raise awareness and build understanding
	• Change preconceptions of key players
	• Obtain valuable feedback and input.

The guidance provided here is based on common practice and experience, but it is important to note that each individual case is likely to be different and your own knowledge of the personalities and issues involved will need to be brought into play when developing your approach.

3.4.1 Securing wider management commitment

The principal outputs from this stage will be:

○ The presentation of plans to key management representatives and groups, as identified

○ The receipt of feedback from key management representatives and groups

○ The evaluation of the level of real commitment secured

○ The identification of further actions required to secure real commitment from all key management representatives and groups

○ The identification of additional barriers and opportunities

○ The revision of plans as a result of input, feedback, conditions and commitments

3.4.1.1 Presenting and communicating

Getting the right message across at this stage is vitally important, as in many cases this will be the first contact parties will have with the project, and the first organisation-wide exposure the project will receive. Thorough preparation and planning are very important, as are pre-communications. Where presentation skills are lacking, or where specialist input will enhance the message delivery, it is worth considering specially bringing in these skills.

In presenting or communicating the material prepared under section 3.3.5, it is necessary to maintain a focus on the tangible benefits which the audience will derive from the project, as well benefits for the organisation as a whole.

At this stage you are looking for real commitment from the management representatives and groups identified, commitment which will help you develop the implementation and operational plans for the EPE system, and provisional commitment for the later stages of the project. In order to secure this commitment, it is possible that you might have to compromise on original plans and timescales, or settle for less extensive commitment.

3.4.1.2 Obtaining feedback

Having presented, you should seek feedback and input into the plans developed. This, potentially, will provide you with additional information and insight, while getting management representatives and groups involved, and giving them the opportunity to shape the process. It might be necessary to provide assurances that feedback will be handled objectively and in confidence, depending on the culture of the organisation and/or the nature of the individuals involved.

Ideally, you will want to obtain feedback in person (or through the presenter), so that you can discuss the points raised, if necessary, and clear up any misunderstanding. In addition, if you obtain feedback at the presentation itself, you receive the information quickly, the quality of the information will be better and response rates are likely to be higher. If you have to use feedback mechanisms remotely or which don't solicit an immediate response, set strict deadlines and be prepared to chase for responses. Offering incentives for prompt and full responses can sometimes facilitate better feedback results, though this adds cost to the process, and might encourage respondents to provide answers which they think you want to hear.

Obtaining feedback should not be treated as a one-way process, or as a one-off. At this stage of the project, you want to be maximising the opportunity to build relationships with key parties, and to enhance the credibility of the project and of the core EPE team. Acknowledging feedback, and initiating dialogue from feedback received, is a good way of starting this process. This approach also helps to make people feel as if they have been listened to and their opinions valued, which will encourage them to buy into the project.

Establish or keep feedback channels open throughout the project, as this makes the core EPE team accessible and can provide valuable inputs. It also removes the need to establish new channels at each communication stage, and allows users to become familiar with the process and format, which in turn can generate a higher quality of feedback.

3.4.1.3 Evaluating commitment

Although commitment may be forthcoming when you present the project proposal, it is worth evaluating how sincere this commitment really is. It is possible that key management members or groups will want to be seen to be supportive in the presence of superiors or peers yet in reality have little interest in the project or intention of fulfilling commitments made. Alternatively, some parties may not raise any issues at this stage but seek to undermine the project in a different forum.

This step of the process will very much be shaped around your own perceptions and instincts, and as such some of your evaluations may well prove to be incorrect. However, failure to recognise when real commitment has not been secured can undermine management efforts, plans and, potentially, the project as whole.

In addition to this it is possible that commitment is given conditionally, on the basis that further activity is completed or requests met.

3.4.1.4 Securing further commitment

Having evaluated the level of commitment secured from the identified management representatives and groups, it will be necessary to plan additional activity where requested, and where a lack of real commitment is suspected.

The nature of any such activity will vary from organisation to organisation, and plan to plan, and can only be decided by you based on the nature of the circumstances.

Some examples of additional activity can be seen in section 2.3.4.

3.4.1.5 Identifying additional barriers and opportunities

From the steps already conducted during this stage, it is possible that additional, unforeseen, barriers and/or opportunities will have arisen. It will be important to identify these, so that project plans can be amended.

3.4.1.6 Revision of project plans

The input and feedback received through this round of presentation and communication, coupled with the identification of further barriers and opportunities, are likely to require that the original plans presented be revised.

Any revision of the project plans will need to consider planned activities, timescales and resource requirements. In addition to this, it will be important to recognise where any revisions will impact upon any commitments made or conditions agreed through presentations and communications.

3.4.2 Agreeing project plans

The principal outputs from this stage will be:

○ Gaining agreement on the revised outline plan from the key management representatives and groups

○ Acknowledging and utilising the commitment given

○ Recording the details of any commitments made or conditions agreed.

3.4.2.1 Agreeing an outline plan

Once the project plans have been revised, in response to the initial round of presentations and communications, it will be necessary to gain agreement on the revised outline plan. The nature of the conditions agreed to for the revision of the plans will very much dictate what approach is required to present the revised plans. However, it will be important to update all the key parties, by some means, on the changes made to the outline plan and the implications of these changes.

Agreement on the outline plan and resource requirements (definite or in principle) must be secured before the project is progressed.

3.4.2.2 Acknowledging and utilising commitment given

With agreement to the revised outline plan gained, it will help to build relationships with the key management representatives and groups if you acknowledge the commitment that they have given to the project. Acknowledgement should follow quickly, once commitment is secured, in order to maintain the momentum of the project, build credibility and avoid other projects or initiatives overtaking the EPE project as a priority.

At its simplest, this acknowledgement might be a short communication expressing your thanks. However, more-effective forms of acknowledgement will often focus on utilising the commitment made. For example:

* The scheduling of further meetings to discuss required actions
* The arrangement of presentations, workshops or seminars for a manager's department or team

- The request for the nomination of team members who will be responsible for, or involved in, the project
- The delegation of some predetermined action points
- An invitation to take specific responsibility within the project.

By immediately attempting to utilise the commitments made, you will ensure that the momentum of the project, from the presentation stage, is maintained, and if managed well, progress towards the EPE project objectives, and more general environmental goals, should be rapid.

In addition to acknowledging commitment, it is also worth considering how you will recognise and reward strong commitment and/or achievement. Given the likely limitations of resources available to you, it will probably be necessary to be creative over the way you reward parties. Any such rewards also need to be recognised as such both by the parties being rewarded and by those who are not, though such situations will need managing carefully so as not to disillusion or distance key parties. Knowing the parties involved will help in identifying the right rewards.

Some examples of possible low-cost rewards are listed below.

- Provision of additional support and training
- Involvement in trials and experimentation
- Publicity through reports and newsletters
- Presentations and awards
- Secondments and exchanges
- Greater involvement in project development.

3.4.2.3 Recording commitments and conditions

In securing commitment and agreement to project plans and resources, it is possible that you, as the project manager, will have had to make some commitments and agree some conditions. Such commitments or conditions, in many cases, will influence the development, implementation and operation of the EPE system at some stage. In view of this, it is important to record clearly any commitments made and/or conditions agreed at this stage, for future reference not only by yourself but by core EPE team members and succeeding project managers or owners. This record should be kept up to date throughout the operation of the EPE system.

The record kept could be in the form of meeting minutes, meeting notes, records of communications (hard copy or electronic) or a bespoke document suited to your project approach.

Section 3.4 checklist

Before you embark on the next stages of EPE implentation you should have:

○   Presented plans to key management representatives and groups, as identifed

○   Revised plans as a result of input, feedback, conditions and commitments

○   Gained agreement on the revised outline plan from the key management representatives and groups

○   Acknowledged commitment given, and established means by which to utilise this commitment

○   Recorded the details of any commitments made or conditions agreed.

Task Heading	**Selecting indicators for EPE**
Section Reference	**3.5**
Duration	2 man days +
Difficulty Rating	3
Aims & Objectives	The aim of this section is to select and develop indicators, which will form the basis of the EPE system, to support the achievement of the goals identified in section 3.3.

By following each stage of this section you will have produced a range of indicators to help you monitor performance at a point or over time, and at different levels within the organisation. |
| Outputs | The principal outputs of this section will be:
- The identification of indicator focus to support stated goals and the needs of interested parties
- The identification of existing indicators
- The selection of potential indicators
- The review of potential indicators
- The testing of initial indicator sets
- A final draft set of indicators. |
Resources Considerations People	Project manager Core EPE team Top management Operational management Supervisory staff Operational and support staff Advisers or consultants Key external interested parties
Physical	Work station and office facilities Meeting facilities Transport and communications Access to information Access to analysis tools Honesty and realism Administrational support Environmental performance indicators suggested or required by government, trade bodies or voluntary agreements
Outputs from Previous Tasks	Commitment from all key management representatives and groups. Section 3.4.2 Agreed outline of resource requirements, timescales and milestones. Section 3.4.2 The direction and goals for the EPE system. Section 3.3.3 An understanding of the role of indicators, their characteristics and categories under ISO14031. Sections 2.2.2 2.2.3 and 2.2.4

Potential Problems	• Lack of clear direction and/or goals • Lack of competencies in the EPE team • Limited availability of reliable information • Over-ambitious range of indicators • Inaccurate assumptions regarding the relationships between variables, aspects and impacts • Limited range of input or feedback.
Potential Opportunities	• Gaining buy-in from interested parties through involvement • Building relationships and trust • Linkages to incentive schemes • Focus on management inputs • Address industry or sector environmental performance indicators • Support for performance tracking, reporting and communications.

3.5.1 Identifying indicator focus

The principal outputs of this stage will be:

O   The identification of the broad environmental topics which need to be addressed by environmental activity

O   The identification of the key interested parties who will required indicator information or whom you want to communicate indicator information to

O   The identification of the sort of indicator information which each interested party will be interested in

O   The identification of any established indicators which address these environmental topics

It is important here to make the point that the selection and use of indicators will help you track environmental performance and provide information which should help you manage this performance – the application of indicators will not, in itself, deliver environmental performance improvement.

In view of this, it is clear that indicators will be useful only as long as they provide valid information on the organisation's key environmental performance areas. Views of interested parties should also be captured within these performance areas and any criteria developed.

Figure 32 illustrates the role of indicators in supporting the achievement of goals, objectives and targets, and subsequently improvements in environmental performance.

Figure 32 **The role of indicators in an organisation (a) with a formal EMS and (b) without a formal EMS**

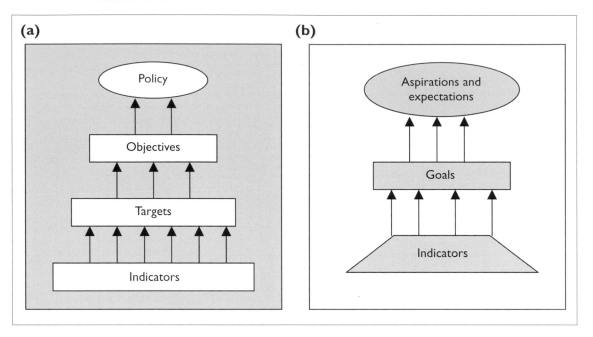

3.5.1.1 **Identifying broad environmental topics**

The work completed so far will have provided you with a clear vision of the aims of the EPE system (section 3.3.3), and a direction and goals for environmental performance improvement activity (section 3.3.2). The identification of broad environmental topics, to be assessed through the use of indicators, should stick closely to these two outputs and the project plans agreed in section 3.4.

If you already have clearly defined environmental performance criteria, or established objectives and targets (under a formal EMS), these will form the basis of your 'broad topic' identification. However, further areas can be included as deemed appropriate.

The following list presents some examples of broad environmental topics:

- Electricity consumption for group
- Water use and discharge from central region operations
- Solid-waste generation in cutting rooms
- Emissions to air by process
- Consumption of raw materials
- Handling, storage and disposal of hazardous and polluting materials
- Implementation of an ISO14001 certifiable EMS
- Evaluation of packaging design
- Legal compliance

- Commercial transport use
- Disposal and recovery of products produced
- Environmental probity of suppliers of raw materials and services
- Impacts of service provision on customers
- Communication with local pressure groups
- The environmental-risk appraisal of operating sites (before and during occupation).

From these examples, you will see that the definition of 'broad topic' will very much depend upon the size and nature of your organisation. The key thing to remember at this stage is not to get too focused on specific areas, as this may over-complicate the identification of potential indicators and obscure some opportunities.

Appendix 16 provides a template for the recording of 'broad environmental topics' (see Figure 33)

3.5.1.2 Identifying the users of indicator information

Once the broad environmental topics have been identified, it will be possible to list parties with specific interest in each of the broad topic areas. Appendix 16 provides space for these interested parties to be recorded against each topic area. The work conducted in section 3.1.3 on identifying interested parties should prove useful at this stage.

In identifying users of indicator information, you should not overlook the environmental management function itself – it is probable that this is where information will be used the most.

Figure 33   Example of identifying users' requirements for indicator information

Broad Environmental Topic	Interested Parties	Indicator Information Requirements
Electricity use	Operational managers & environmental manager	Detailed breakdown of kilowatt/hour usage and cost, by activity and shift.
	Operations director	Detailed breakdown of kilowatt/hour usage and cost, by operating centre.
	Procurement team	Detailed breakdown of kilowatt/hour usage by product unit produced.
	Government bodies	Total CO_2 emissions, including those related to electricity usage.
	Investors	Total cost of energy consumed and financial exposure to increased duties, levies and market-price fluctuations.

(Shortened version of Appendix 16)

3.5.1.3 Identifying the information requirements of users

Each of the parties identified in the previous stage (including the environmental management function) is likely to have different information needs and will require information expressed in ways that mean something to them. At this stage it will be useful to identify, at a general level, the information requirements of each interested party, under each broad topic area (using Appendix 16).

Some information may have been collected during the work conducted in section 3.1.3 which might help in identifying information needs. If not, it may be necessary to revisit this work, and approach interested parties to find out what their information requirements are. If you have to do this, take care to manage the expectations of the parties approached as to the information they will eventually receive, given that you might not be able to meet all of their expectations.

3.5.1.4 Identifying established indicators

At this stage it will be useful to identify what (if any) indicators are already in use within your organisation, or as established industry measures, which relate to the topic areas identified. This will save you from developing these indicators again, or developing overlapping indicators, which could increase the collection and analysis burden and potentially confuse users. If you are considering externally applied indicators, there are potential publicity and benchmarking benefits to be gained by adopting such approaches.

It is worth noting that indicators might exist which are not identified as environmental performance indicators, or as the result of any environmental management activity.

Some examples of indicators which might currently exist are listed below.

* Data on resource consumption, such as materials purchasing records, utility invoices and meter readings, compared with measures of business activity, such as units of production or man hours
* Financial information on environmental services bought in over a period of time, or related to a level of business activity
* Measures of environmental incidents, either by some form of severity rating, or by clean-up costs or legal-action costs
* Fuel consumption per mile or kilometre for vehicles
* Parts lifetime for machinery or vehicles, expressed against a unit of activity, such as the mile, or tonne produced, meter printed, etc.
* Financial investment in environmental projects per site

- Percentage of management time devoted to environmental management activity
- Percentage carton fill in packing process.

Indicators thus identified could be used directly in final indicator sets, or might provide information which can be converted for use in a different indicator format. Whichever way, the use of existing indicators can save time and resources, as well as providing an accepted base around which to introduce new measures. The use of external indicators can be particularly useful, as this will directly address the needs of some key interested parties.

3.5.2 Selecting and developing indicators

The principal outputs from this section will be:

O   The identification of potential indicators and indicator sets

O   The identification of data requirements for potential indicators

When selecting and developing indicators be mindful of the resource and competence limitations of the project, both during implementation and for ongoing operation.

Before you begin to tackle this section it might prove useful to review sections 2.2.3 and 2.2.4, which look at the characteristics and categories of indicators as defined in ISO14031.

3.5.2.1 Identifying potential indicators

Having identified the broad environmental topic areas that you want to address with the EPE system, and highlighted the principal interested parties and their information requirements, the next stage will be to identify potential indicators which will provide the necessary information.

The example in Figure 33, shows that in many cases the information required by different stakeholders under one topic is often very similar and can be derived from a few sets of data if collected in great enough detail. Given this, it is advisable when developing indicators to try to build them from common data sets. This approach will reduce the amount of data which need collecting, communicating, handling, storing and verifying, which in turn will reduce resource and time requirements.

The ranges of indicators developed from base sets of data streams are referred to as indicator sets. Within each indicator set there will be a hierarchy of indicators, which builds up from the most detailed level of indicators at the bottom, to overall indicators at the top.

Figure 34   An illustration of the hierarchy of indicators within an indicator set

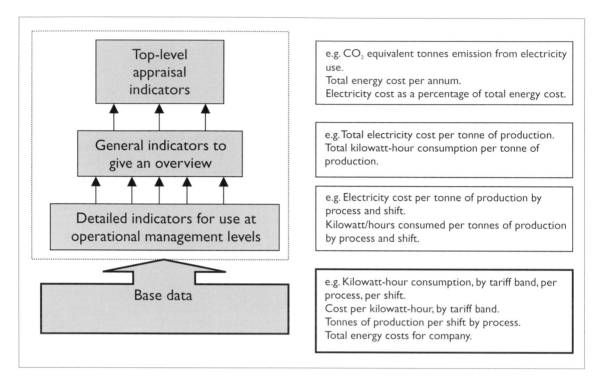

In selecting potential indicators, you will need to address the information requirements identified for each interested party. In addition to this, to assist you with comparability, you should try to maintain some consistency in the base-data requirements and terms of expression used. If we refer to the examples in Figure 34, all the indicators developed could be derived from the base data collected, and all indicators are related to tonnes of production.

The terms of expression used need to be understood by, and be in line with the expectations of, the intended audience. This might call for the use of some conversion factors and/or further base-data streams.

Appendix 16 provides space to develop potential indicators for each interested party, and Appendix 17 provides a template on which to record the profile of each indicator, which will become the main reference point for indicator details from now on (see Figure 35).

At this stage it will probably be helpful to develop a referencing system for the indicators you develop, to avoid confusion at a later stage.

3.5.2.2   Identifying data requirements for potential indicators

Having identified potential environmental indicators, the next step will be to identify data sets which would be required to calculate these indicators.

Data sets identified should be, or at least potentially be, measurable in a consistent and reliable manner. At this stage, it is worth taking an open perspective on what can be measured, even if this measurement is not possible at the time. This will help you focus on obtaining the most suitable data rather than making do, and will lead you to seek opportunities to obtain these data. Ultimately, obtaining the data may not be possible, but it is better to keep options open at this stage. If you are unsure of the possibilities, identifying some alternative or proxy measures as contingencies would be advisable. Any proxy measures adopted must be relevant to the indicator in question.

Potential data sets identified will generally fall into six types:

- Actual measured data, relating to an environmental aspect, impact or condition
- Estimated data, provided in the absence of actual measured data
- Calculated data, derived from actual measured data or estimated data according to a defined calculation method
- Proxy data, which approximate to a different, immeasurable, data stream
- Relative data, which relate to variable factors which can influence an environmental aspect, impact or condition, e.g. units of production
- Conversion data, which relate to a factor which is used for converting actual data into a term of expression, e.g. the cost of a tonne of material.

For example, a cleaning contractor wants to assess detergent use in relation to floor surface area cleaned. Two data streams identified for this indicator are:

- Actual: The volume of detergent used
- Relative: The surface area of floors cleaned in a week.

If the contractor wants to assess the cost of detergent in relation to floor surface cleaned, then he would need to collect data on the cost per litre of detergent used, which would be conversion data.

In the event that data on actual volumes used are not available, then a proxy measure might be the amount spent on detergent, or the quantity of containers disposed of. In the event that data on the surface area of floors cleaned in a week are not available, then a proxy measure might be man hours, or number of mops issued.

As can be seen from the example, proxy measures are rarely as reliable as the direct measure, given that they are approximations, but in some cases they allow the evaluation of otherwise immeasurable data.

In this example, the proxy measures identified may actually be useful in their own right as actual measures. It should be remembered that there are many ways of assessing environmental performance under one indicator set, the desirability of each depending upon the audience who will receive the indicator information.

When identifying the data streams to be measured, some other factors need to considered as well:

- Timing, when are data collected and how often?
- Location, where are data collected?
- Scope, what data are included?
- Units of measurement, what units are data sets recorded in?

All of these considerations are important, as they will determine the level of detail of the data collected. While you may not be seeking a great level of detail initially, you should consider the benefits gained from detailed data collection when it comes to identifying root causes. Trying to obtain detailed data retrospectively is likely to be very difficult, resource intensive and/or costly, whereas consolidating data is relatively easy as long as measurement is consistent.

Figure 35 provides an example of indicator-detail recording for the cleaning company scenario above, using the template presented in Appendix 17.

Figure 35   Example of considerations when identifying data measures

Mopper's Cleaning Services						
Indicator Reference	Set	RM	Indicator	22 / 2000		
Indicator Details	Quantity of detergent used per square metre of floor area cleaned					
Topic Area	Cleaning-material consumption					
Interested Parties	Managing Director Operational management Environmental management Cleaners					
Intended Purpose	To track detergent use and provide information to manage the reduction of detergent used, saving money and reducing environmental impacts.					
Data Required	Timing	Location	Scope	Unit	Reference	Type
Quantity of detergent issued	Weekly	By cleaner	Floor cleaner only	Litre	FC235679/234	A
	Data Source		Gang supervisor materials and equipment issues log			
Floor surface area cleaned	Weekly	By cleaner	Hard floor surfaces only	Square Metre	N/A	R
	Data Source		Gang supervisors weekly job report			
ISO14031 Description						
Category	Operational performance indicator		Characteristic	Relative		
Additional Notes	Floor cleaner also used on work surfaces and tiled splash backs. These are not included in floor surface area calculations.					

Key to type abbreviations:

A = Actual, E = Estimated, C = Calculated, P = Proxy, R = Relative, X = Conversion

(Shortened example of Appendix 17)

Note that the timing and location of data sampling, for actual and relative measures, have been kept consistent. While this may not always be possible, it is advisable to try to achieve it, as it will aid comparability of data.

Where there is any doubt over the accuracy or reliability of the data stream identified, it is worth noting such concerns at this stage, for future reference. Similarly, if you can identify the source of data at this stage, it is worth completing the 'data source' section, to save unnecessary work in the next stages.

3.5.3   Reviewing potential indicators

The principal outputs from this section will be:

○   The assessment of the practicality of potential indicators

○   The assessment of the relevance of potential indicators

○   The identification of actions required to implement potential indicators

○   The testing of potential indicators

○   The identification of a final draft set of indicators.

3.5.3.1   Assessing practicality

From identifying potential indicators, it will now be necessary to assess whether they are practical within your organisation. Where indicators are adopted from other schemes, this stage will be of particular relevance. Appendix 17 provides space under the 'data required' section to identify the potential source(s) of the data. Further notes can be added in the notes section provided.

Identifying required data is one thing, obtaining them is another. Some assessment of data availability may have been made in the previous stage, but where a more open approach has been adopted, assessing the availability of data will be necessary. In addition to this you might have identified some data-collection practices in section 3.2.1.

In many organisations, a large amount of data are available, especially when they relate to financial transactions, or resource inputs or outputs. The data may not be collated and reported routinely, but can probably be obtained on request, and routine collation could be established with little or no extra effort. The increasing use of electronic data-management systems is quickly making more and more data readily available in numerous formats and terms of expression.

Data which have been identified as useful in EPE may not be recognised as environmental management information, and as such will exist under a number of different headings and departments. In view of this, it will probably be necessary to ask around within the organisation to see if relevant information exists.

Figure 36 provides an example of the variety of sources of data, in seeking data relating to product pack weights.

Figure 36   **Example of sources of pack weight data**

Source of Data	Nature of Data
Production	Pallet configuration details
Pack labels	Pack weights printed on labels
Quality assurance	Quality inspection check weighing records
Sales	Product specification data sheets
Design	Product design specification
Storage and handling	Inventory management system
Distribution	Load planning, weight distribution calculations
Site security	Weighbridge records

In this example, there would appear to be a number of sources of the same data. You will need to assess which source provides the most reliable data in the format that most conveniently fits your timescale, location, scope and unit of measure criteria. The cost of obtaining the data may also be a consideration, though if they already exist this is likely to less important. It is worth remembering that data can also be obtained from sources outside the organisation, although in some instances cost could be a significant factor.

Some potential sources of data are listed, for your reference, in Figure 37.

Figure 37   **Potential sources of data for EPE**

Accounts payable	Distribution
Personal expenses	Planning
Human resources	Project teams
Marketing	Public relations department
Sales	Contractors
Product design	Suppliers
Research and development	Customers
Production	Trade bodies
Purchasing	Industry surveys
Customer services	Environment agency
Operations	Local authority
Stores and warehousing	Government information
IT department	Non-government organisations
Facilities and site services	Publicly available information

Where data are not available in your chosen format, it is worth investigating what proxy data might exist. While proxy data are unlikely to be as good as the actual data, they can provide a more cost-effective option for getting an indication of environmental performance.

If you choose to establish new data-gathering processes (which will probably be required at some stage), then you will need to evaluate the resource and timescale implications of this. It will be important to assess whether the cost of implementing new practices, involving as it may the overcoming of structural barriers, is justified by the value of the data obtained. Further, cultural barriers can exist which should also be taken into account. Figure 38 identifies some common structural and cultural barriers which should be considered when assessing the development of new data-gathering procedures and practices.

Figure 38   Potential barriers to establishing data collection

Structural	Cultural
Lack of skills, competencies and understanding Lack of suitable equipment or materials Lack of time No opportunity to collate accurate data Existing data-collection practices and procedures are substandard	Lack of real commitment, data collection is seen as being of secondary importance Resistance to new ways of working Resistance to increased work load Suspicion of measurement and monitoring Distortion of data, especially where subjective evaluations are required

In addition to assessing practicality, in terms of data availability, it is also worth considering the volume of data that will be generated and the ability to handle, process, analyse, verify and store them. The method by which data are recorded and communicated will influence your capability effectively to handle them and the availability of data-processing equipment and labour input will also be significant.

Where large amounts of data are to be collected, it might be possible to implement basic data-processing practices at the point and time of collection. This can spread the workload and ensure that data are communicated in a manageable format. On the other hand, it can cause resentment and will require tighter controls and verification.

The complexity of data needs to be considered as well. In some instances you will find that data are collected in the format you require, yet these data are then heavily converted or manipulated to meet other requirements, and the base data are lost or obscured. Unravelling the end result to obtain the original data can often be time consuming, and when approximations and rounding factors have been applied in conversion, the data can end up being unreliable.

Reliability of data is another important consideration when assessing practicality: data may well be currently available but if they are unreliable you must question whether they will serve the needs of the EPE system. Be warned, that if you are attempting to track performance, and particularly if you rely on information for reporting purposes, the reliability of the data is very important.

Finally, in addition to assessing the practicality of handling data, consider the practicality of handling the full range of indicators developed. A wide range of indicators may well give you a thorough coverage of environmental performance issues, but will you be able to use this level of information in practice, or will a smaller number of key indicators suffice?

3.5.3.2 Assessing relevance

Having assessed the practicality of the potential indicators developed, it will be necessary to assess whether they are really relevant. It is worth considering whether the interested parties identified will really use all of the indicator information provided, whether there are gaps in important areas and whether the terms of expression are really suitable. Most importantly of all you must assess whether the potential indicators identified will really help you achieve your goals, objectives and targets.

3.5.3.3 Identifying actions to implement potential indicators

From assessing the practicality and relevance of the potential indicators, you should have been able to identify the indicators that will form the basis of the EPE system. The aim of this stage is to identify what actions are required in order to implement these indicators within the organisation.

At this stage, actions will need to cover:

* Collection of data
* Handling and storage of data
* Initial conversion of data
* Communication of data.

Appendix 17 provides space for recording the necessary actions required under each indicator. It will be useful to identify, where possible, any resource and cost implications, as well as identifying any significant barriers (or opportunities) that might present themselves.

In addition to this, the template provides space to enter details of procedures for the collection of data, any initial processing, and the communication of data. This will be required in most cases where new or amended data-gathering practices are to be introduced, to facilitate the establishment of data collection.

3.5.3.4 Testing potential indicators

Depending on the nature of the potential indicators developed, or the data requirements, it might be necessary or desirable to test the practicality and reliability of the indicators prior to selecting the first draft indicator sets.

Some hints for the testing of potential indicators are listed below for your reference.

* Select a representative and manageable sample to test
* Predict the results you expect from the test by which to compare actual outputs
* Conduct more than one test, to ascertain reliability and consistency
* Try to conduct tests at little or no extra cost to the organisation
* Try to conduct tests over a short timescale, so that they do not become the main focus of the project
* Try to conduct tests in line with predicted methodology
* Involve data collectors, data handlers and interested parties in the testing process, and obtain feedback from them
* Test indicators retrospectively, using historical data, where this can be achieved, for speed and to keep costs down
* Identify problem areas and significant influencing factors, and decide on remedial action or revisions to indicator format

Remember that this stage is only for testing potential indicators, and you need to be careful not to allow it to become too drawn out or costly. Indicators can always be taken out or included during the operation of the EPE system.

3.5.3.5 Establishing the final draft indicator set

Having completed all of the stages of this section, you should be in a position to select the final draft set of indicators that will form the basis of your EPE system. This set of indicators should support the vision of the EPE, and the direction and goals established (developed in section 3.3). The indicators selected should be practicable, reliable and manageable.

Appendix 18 presents a template for the summarisation of the indicators selected as part of the final draft, and provides space to reference across to the indicator profiles developed using Appendix 17. Mapping the indicator sets with data flows might also prove useful, to gain an overview of how the indicators selected fit together and discover whether there are any significant gaps in the structure.

Section 3.5 checklist

Before you embark on the next stages of EPE implementation you should have:

○ Identified the broad environmental topics which need to be addressed by environmental activity

○ Identified the key interested parties who will require indicator information, or who you want to communicate indicator information to

○ Identified the sort of indicator information which each interested party will be interested in

○ Identifed potential indicators and indicator sets

○ Identified data requirements for potential indicators

○ Assessed the practicality and relevance of potential indicators

○ Identified actions required to implement indicators

○ Identified a final draft set of indicators.

Task Heading	**Producing an implementation plan**
Section Reference	**3.6**
Duration	5 man days +
Difficulty Rating	4
Aims & Objectives	The aim of this section is to create a detailed plan for putting the EPE system in place.
	By following each stage of this section you will have developed a detailed implementation plan which identifies resource requirements, specific tasks, timescales, milestones, reviews and feedback.
Outputs	The principal outputs of this section will be:
	• The identification of all the actions required to enable the collection, communication, analysis, assessment, storage and reporting of reliable data
	• The identification of targets and timescales for completing all actions
	• The identification of resources required to achieve the actions within the timescales set, with rationale for any variances from previous agreements
	• Rationale for any variation between new and previously agreed plans
	• The identification of people who will be responsible for actions
	• The development of detailed project 'initiation' activity - including awareness raising, presentation of the rationale, training and support material, systems implementation and provision of assistance
	• An implementation plan report summarising the outputs from this section.
Resources Considerations	
People	Project manager
	Project team
	Functional and operational management
	Supervisory staff
	Operational and support staff
	Advisers and consultants
Physical	Work station and office facilities
	Meeting facilities
	Transport and communications
	Project-planning information or software packages
	Administrational support
Outputs from Previous Tasks	The vision of what the EPE system will deliver. Section 3.3.3
	Results of analysis of the practicality of applying initial indicators. Section 3.5.3
	Test results from initial indicator sets. Section 3.5.3
	Final draft set of indicators. Section 3.5.3
	Evaluation of the level of commitment secured. Section 3.4.1.3
	Identification of barriers to EPE system implementation. Section 3.4.1.5
	Agreed outline of resource requirements, timescales and milestones. Section 3.4.2.1
	List of commitments made and/or conditions agreed. Section 3.4.2.3
	A plan of required activity to ensure real commitment is secured. Section 3.4.1.4

Potential Problems	• Lack of resources, people or time
	• Lack of input and commitment from key players
	• Lack of competencies
	• Over-ambitious projections
	• Adherence to unrealistic commitments
	• Limited range of input or feedback.
Potential Opportunities	• Building relationships and confidence
	• Gaining buy-in from interested parties through involvement
	• Utilisation of commitment secured from key management representatives
	• Incorporation of valuable features of the organisation to assist implementation.

3.6.1   Identifying implementation activity

The principal outputs from this stage will be:

O   Reviewing actions for intitial data collection and handling

O   Identifying actions for data analysis, assessment and verification

O   Identifying actions for information reporting

O   Identifying actions for establishing a review process with feedback channels

O   The development of procedures and the defining of practices

O   Identifying likely communications, information and training requirements

O   Identifying check-back and auditing activity to ensure that the EPE system implementation is meeting expectations.

3.6.1.1   Reviewing actions for initial data collection and handling

In section 3.5.3.3 we identified the required actions for the initial collection and handling of data for each indicator developed. It will be worth reviewing the detail of these actions for the first draft indicator set developed, to ensure that they are still feasible and valid in light of testing and any other changes. Communications requirements may well be different for implementation and operation than they are for the testing of indicators, and these actions might need redefining once the analysis tasks have been identified and positioned in the organisation.

At this stage it might be useful to start compiling an activity list and identifying approximate deadlines for completion. This will assist you in prioritising the range of activities when, later in this section, you look at setting timescales and targets, and begin preparing detailed implementation plans.

If you can identify activities that are dependent on the completion of other activities as well, this will further assist you in future tasks.

3.6.1.2 Identifying actions for data analysis, assessment and verification

Once data have been collected and any initial conversion has taken place, they will need communicating to a point for analysis. As mentioned in the previous stage (3.6.1.1), the actions required for analysis to be established will probably influence the communication requirements.

You will need to provide adequate facilities, equipment and materials to enable analysts to receive, handle, convert, interrogate and store the data supplied. These provisions will need to be sufficient to enable analysts to handle the quantities of data proposed, and produce output within allowed timescales. Note that data and information date quickly, so fast and efficient approaches are preferable.

In addition to this, the individuals responsible for the analysis of data will require certain skills, so training and support could be required. If such capability does not exist within the organisation, it might be decided to out-source the analysis work.

Note that this guidebook makes the distinction between data and information as follows:

* Data are collected and are applied to specified indicators at the analysis stage
* The outputs from the indicators are information, along with any other outputs from the analysis process.

Assessment of information will often be carried out by the analysts, but if different skills or understanding are required, then this may be the task of others. Similar considerations need to be given here as for the analysis and conversion of data.

Verification requirements will also be similar, but here you should consider how verification will be performed – for example, by exception, as a reaction, or as part of a scheduled routine. The individuals you use to verify data may not be the analysts or assessors, and these individuals will need certain competencies, along with access to resources and equipment, to enable them to reach the data-collection points and conduct meaningful verifications.

3.6.1.3 Identifying actions for information reporting

Information provided from analysis, assessment and verification will then be available for communication internally, and externally if so desired. The methods of communication envisaged will probably vary according to the audience targeted, and to the nature and quantity of information being communicated. Given this, the actions required to ensure information reporting will vary greatly.

In section 3.5 we identified the interested parties for each broad topic area and built indicators around this to meet the needs of those parties. This should form the basis of your work on identifying how you will report information from the EPE system. Some steps are listed below for you to consider when approaching this.

* Identify the information and terms of expression required for all targeted interested parties
* Identify the reporting intervals
* Identify the media which you will use to communicate the information to interested parties
* Identify the mode of delivery (e.g. post, electronic, personal presentation)
* Assess the relative costs of different approaches
* Assess the lead-time, or speed, of different approaches.

The decisions on what approach to take should consider the levels of understanding of the interested parties, preferences for different modes of communication, and the ability to manage and utilise the information provided. The assessment of cost is important, given that some modes of communication can be expensive and if performed regularly could place an unrealistic burden on the EPE system. Also remember that information depreciates in value to the user over time, so the quicker you can get it to the interested parties the better (in most cases).

It might be useful to think of information as a product which needs to be in the:

* Right PLACE
* At the right TIME
* And in the right CONDITION.

Individuals and groups responsible for preparing information for reporting will require appropriate competencies and knowledge, along with adequate facilities, equipment, materials and time. In some cases it might be worth considering outsourcing this activity, especially when specialist media and modes of delivery are being used.

3.6.1.4 Identifying actions for establishing a review process

The review processes are an important part of the whole EPE system, and as such actions need to be identified which will ensure that reviews are conducted in line with schedules and timescales.

Review forums will need scheduling at regular intervals and communicating to all relevant parties who will have input. Facilities should be available to enable these forums to take place, along with time allocation for attendees to prepare and to follow up agreed actions. Support may be required for aspects of the review such as minute taking, and circulation and dissemination of outputs.

Establishing feedback channels for the review process will necessary, if the review forums are going to address actual issues. These can be set up to coincide with scheduled reviews, although more-effective channels are those which are available for use at any time. Ongoing feedback channels will probably require different facilities to one-off or scheduled feedback approaches.

Appendix 19 provides a template for a review process structure.

3.6.1.5 Developing procedures and defining practices

Many of the actions identified so far will probably involve changes for the individuals involved in implementing and operating the EPE system. In view of this it is advisable to define practices required by the system and provide procedures for training and reference. This will be especially important when dealing with complex operations or where the competencies of individuals or groups do not match the requirements of the task.

Note that it may be possible to adopt existing procedures and practices with little or no alteration.

Procedures can be documented and presented in any manner of format, but it is wise to try to develop them in such a manner that they can be easily understood and clearly highlight critical stages of the process. Flowchart style presentation of procedures is often effective, and these can be enhanced through the use of pictures, diagrams, plans, charts, maps, colour and different typefaces. If the procedure will be used as work instruction at the point of activity, make sure that it is practical for use in the environment and conditions likely to be encountered. For instance, if you are dipping a tank in the yard, procedures on a poster may not be very practical for the operator.

3.6.1.6 Identifying likely communications, information and training requirements

This stage may not be possible to complete in detail until individuals have been identified later in this section, but it will probably be possible to identify communications, information and training that will be required to implement the EPE system.

Initial communications will almost certainly be required for all individuals and groups who will be affected by the project, and it might also be desirable to inform other parties as well. These communications will launch the project and EPE system across the organisation and will also convey important information to raise awareness, build knowledge and possibly instruct.

Communications can take many forms, from remote mail shots and notices, through to one to one briefings. What the best approach is will depend upon the audience, the information being communicated, cost and time restrictions and the culture of the organisation.

Specific training sessions and communications should be arranged to support and complement each other. Activities related to training will include:

- The preparation of material
- The scheduling of training
- Communication with attendees
- Arrangement of facilities, equipment, materials and support
- The provision of feedback mechanisms
- The provision of flexibility in the schedule and resources plans to accommodate additional training, instruction and support.

3.6.1.7 Identifying check-back and auditing activity

Amidst all of the implementation activity identified, it will be necessary to check back and audit practices, procedures and equipment once the implementation has begun. By doing this you will be able quickly to assess:

- How well the implementation programme is progressing against established timescales and milestones
- Any shortfall in commitment
- The level of provision of resources and time
- Any unforeseen difficulties or problems
- Further requirements for information, training and support
- The effectiveness of the feedback mechanisms established
- The degree of reliability and consistency of data and information

- The morale of the individuals and groups involved in the implementation programme
- Any potential opportunities presented.

Check backs and auditing at the implementation level may form part of an ongoing auditing process or be restricted purely to the implementation phase and the verifying of the success of the implementation. Whichever way, it is advisable to check as many elements of the implementation as possible: this will ensure that weak links in the system are more likely to be detected early, and will also help to build relationships, morale and commitment among the people involved, if done in a supportive manner.

3.6.2 Planning the implementation process

The principal outputs from this stage will be:

○ The establishment of project targets and timescales

○ The identification of implementation resource requirements

○ An assessment of resource and timescale variations from project plans agreed (see sections 2.3.4 and 3.4.2)

○ Identifying implementation responsibilities

○ Identifying the implementation team(s)

○ An analysis of training and knowledge-building requirements for the implementation team

3.6.2.1 Establishing project targets and timescales

Having identified all of the activities which will be required for the implementation of the EPE system, it will necessary now to put these activities into a timeframe and establish some targets for completion of tasks and the quality of implementation. The project plans developed earlier on will provide a useful reference point for this activity (see sections 2.3.4 and 3.4.2).

It was mentioned in section 3.6.1.1 that you might find it useful to record each activity, the likely duration and any dependency on other activities. If you did not record this information, you will need to address this before you can plan the activities into a time schedule. At this stage, timescale prediction needs to be as accurate as possible, especially if you are seeking to move the programme along quickly. If you are unsure of the timescale requirements, it will be best to find out before planning in too much activity around this.

When seeking final approval and commitment, it is likely that management will be looking for precise timescale detail so they can calculate the effect this might have on their areas. As part of the process of identifying timescales for completing tasks, it can prove valuable to note any assumptions made in the calculation of the timescales.

Appendix 2, as used for the preparation of the outline plan, might prove useful as a template for planning implementation activity. Alternatively, you may prefer to design a format which is capable of containing more detail. As with the outline planning stage in section 2.3.2, it might be necessary to consider some resource issues when scheduling activities. In view of this, it might be worth tackling this stage in conjunction with the next stage, 3.6.2.2.

Establishing targets for the implementation process will provide the implementation team with a focus throughout, and milestones by which to measure performance. Targets can be determined before, during or after the timescale scheduling, as appropriate, though they should take into account any project goals stated, commitments made or conditions imposed in securing management commitment.

At this stage it is possible (if this has not been done at the identification of indicators stage (section 3.5)) to establish some indicators to track the performance of the implementation of the EPE system itself. These might provide useful benchmarks, and allow for more-objective and more-quantitative targeting. Some examples of possible areas to consider when establishing such indicators are listed below.

- Completion of scheduled activities to timescales
- Level of feedback obtained
- Results of check backs and audits
- Rating of training delivered
- Expenditure on the project against projections
- Time committed to implementation by employees and contractors
- Rating of reliability for data produced
- Amount of indicators operational
- Quality rating of reports
- Timeliness of reports against schedule
- Savings or revenues generated as a result of project-implementation activity
- Employee satisfaction surveys.

The establishment of indicators for the monitoring of achievement in the implementation phase should not be confused with the indicators established as the main thrust of the EPE system. Implementation indicators only help you track performance in implementing the EPE system, not the organisation's actual environmental performance.

3.6.2.2 Identifying implementation resource requirements

Much of the guidance provided in section 2.3.3.1 will apply in identifying resource requirements for the implementation programme. The difference at this stage will be that the level of detail will need to be much greater, with each activity assessed and costed. The list of examples provided in section 2.3.3.1 may well help you identify resources required.

It will be worth identifying individuals, groups or positions in relation to labour input at this stage. This will include implementation project team members, administrators, trainers, auditors, analysts and assessors, down to data collectors and communicators.

3.6.2.3 An assessment of resource and timescale variations

Once timescales have been established and resources identified for the implementation of the EPE system, it will be valuable to review these against predictions made in the project plans last agreed by management.

It is unlikely that these will match, and therefore it will probably be required that you justify any variances, especially where these show an increase in cost, resource commitment and/or timescales. Where savings can be identified you will have to weigh up whether it is worth highlighting these, offsetting them against areas of overspend or building them back into the resource plans as contingency or for flexibility.

This stage is very important, as excessively adverse variations could threaten the whole project, and failure to disclose (or realise) likely costs could lead to conflict and problems in the future.

3.6.2.4 Identifying implementation responsibilities and teams

Through identifying actions and resource requirements, it is probable that you will have built up an idea of responsibilities, and levels within the organisation at which these will occur, under the implementation stage.

You will need to identify specific responsibilities for activities within the implementation plan, and from this identify individuals, groups or positions which will be responsible for ensuring action is taken on time and in accordance with programme requirements.

In a similar way to the way it was suggested that you create a core EPE team in section 2.3.5, it is advisable to establish an implementation team or teams. In establishing these teams it will be necessary to assess the competencies and skills possessed by the potential team members, and see if these match the requirements of the implementation phase. This will also apply to individuals identified as responsible for elements of the plan who might not be recognised as part of the implementation team. The template provided in Appendix 4 could be applied for the training-needs analysis at this stage.

In some circumstances the implementation team will be the same as the core EPE team, but it is worth considering whether changes need to be made to bring in individuals with specific skills that will be required during implementation.

3.6.3   Drawing up the implementation plan

The principal outputs from this stage will be:

O   Detailing the project 'initiation' plan

O   Detailing the full implementation plan.

Once all of the previous stages have been completed it will be necessary to draw up a plan for the implementation of the EPE system. This can be used as a tool for managing the implementation as well as providing details of the approach for presentation and communication with key management representatives and groups.

3.6.3.1   Detailing the project 'initiation' plan

The 'initiation' plan is distinct from the overall implementation plan and covers all of the communication, presentation and training activity which must precede the overall implementation activities for the EPE system. The reason for splitting this out from the main plan is that it forms a crucial part of the whole project and as such cannot afford to be overlooked or hidden in the mass of the overall plan.

The 'initiation' will be the first contact most people in the organisation (or outside) will have with the EPE system and project team or teams, and in view of this it needs to be well planned and prepared, and to deliver the right messages, information and training to motivate those involved. If the initiation fails in this, then making the EPE system work will be very much more difficult.

The detail of the initiation should have been identified already, so the nature and content of communications, presentations and training sessions will merely need developing. However, you may want to review timescales to ensure that the initiation plan will not be too drawn out, as this will inevitably affect the momentum of the project and probably disillusion individuals who may have originally been committed.

The initiation plan is aimed at gaining commitment and support from all the people who will be involved, so the style and content of the proposal will be dependent upon the expectations of the group or individual whom you will need to convince. You will need to gear the proposal to highlight the areas of interest for the audience as well as management, and in a style which is acceptable to and easily understood by them.

Some key questions which are likely to be foremost in the minds of the individuals who will be involved are:

- What impact will this have on me or my department?
- What benefits will the project deliver? or, why do we need it?
- How much will it cost? or, what support will be provided?
- How long will it take? or, is this a one off, or ongoing?

You should make the answers to these questions stand out for the audience, along with other answers as deemed necessary for your organisation.

3.6.3.2 **Preparing the full implementation plan**

The detail of the full implementation plan will have been developed through the stages of this section, so this stage will require the preparation of the plan in a presentable and usable format.

Section 3.6 checklist

Before you embark on the next stages of EPE implementation you should have:

O   Established project targets and timescales

O   Identified implementation resource requirements

O   Assessed resource and timescale variations from project plans agreed

O   Identified implementation responsibilities

O   Identified the implementation team or teams

O   Analysed training and knowledge-building requirements

O   Detailed the project 'inititation' plan and the full implementation plan.

Task Heading	**Preparing an operational plan**
Section Reference	**3.7**
Duration	3 man days +
Difficulty Rating	3
Aims & Objectives	The aim of this section is to create an outline plan for the ongoing operation of the EPE system. By following each stage of this section you will have developed an outline operational plan which identifies resource requirements, specific tasks, timescales, milestones, reviews and feedback. In addition you will have prepared a presentation package for key management representatives and groups in order to gain commitment to the implementation and operational plans.
Outputs	• Identification of an individual with overall responsibility for the EPE system • Identification of recurring activities from those identified under section 3.6.1 • A schedule of recurring activities with deadlines and responsibilities • The identification of resources required to facilitate the operation of the EPE system • Identification of personnel with designated responsibility for operational aspects of the EPE system • Identification of additional training and support requirements • A schedule for reporting information generated from the EPE system • A structure and schedule for reviewing feedback on the EPE system • A structured plan of maintenance and improvement for the EPE system • Presentation and support material to facilitate securing management commitment for the implementation and operational plans.
Resources Considerations **People**	Project manager Project team Functional and operational management Operational and support staff Advisers and consultants
Physical	Work station and office facilities Transport and communications Project-planning information and tools Access to information Access to presentation materials
Outputs from Previous Tasks	The implementation plan report. Section 3.6.3 The vision of what the EPE system will deliver for the organisation. Section 3.3.3 Final draft set of indicators. Section 3.5.3.5 Identification of barriers to EPE system implementation. Section 3.4.1.5 List of commitments made and/or conditions agreed. Section 3.4.2.3 Agreed outline of resource requirements, timescales and milestones. Section 3.4.2.1

Potential Problems	• Lack of resources, people or time • Lack of input and commitment from key players • Lack of competencies • Over-ambitious projections • Adherence to unrealistic commitments • Limited range of input or feedback.
Potential Opportunities	• Building relationships and confidence • Gaining buy-in from interested parties through involvement • Utilisation of commitment secured from key management representatives • Incorporation of valuable features of the organisation to assist implementation.

3.7.1 Establishing recurring tasks and responsibilities

The principal outputs from this stage will be:

○ The identification of the person with overall responsibility for the ongoing operation of the EPE system (system owner)

○ The identification of recurring and new activities

○ The establishment of operational responsibilities

○ The establishment of operational teams.

3.7.1.1 Identifying the system owner

In most cases the person responsible for the implementation of the project will be the initial system owner beyond implementation. However, if this is not the case then a suitable individual should be identified at this stage to take on this responsibility.

Identifying this individual at this stage will allow time to plan any training that may be required and also to provide for some form of handover. If it is the intention to appoint a system owner beyond the implementation phase, but no individual can be identified at this stage, then an estimate of required training and induction time will be necessary.

3.7.1.2 Identifying recurring and new activities

Many of the actions identified as required under the implementation plan will be relevant to the ongoing operation of the EPE system as well. These activities are referred to as recurring activities, as opposed to 'one off' activities, which are only required upon implementation (and infrequently if at all beyond this). Figure 39 gives some examples.

Figure 39 Examples of recurring and 'one-off' activities

Recurring Activities	'One Off' Activities
Collection of data	Initial training for data-collection operatives
Analysis of data	Provision of data-analysis software
Verification of data	Check backs on implementation
Reporting of data	Establishment of an intranet location for hosting report information
Review meetings	Identification of review-forum members
EPE news bulletins	EPE 'initiation' communications
Calibration of emissions-monitoring equipment	Procurement and installation of measuring equipment
Soliciting and reviewing feedback	Setting up feedback channels for all employees

(Note: 'one off' activities can recur, but they do not do so on a frequent or routine basis.)

In addition to these recurring activities, it is possible that the ongoing operation will require some new actions to be taken (be they recurring or one off), such as refresher training for data-collection operatives. These new activities will need identifying, along with the recurring activities, for scheduling into the EPE system.

3.7.1.3 The establishment of operational responsibilities and teams

As with the implementation plan (see section 3.6.2.4), it will be necessary to establish the operational responsibilities within the EPE system. These will probably differ from the responsibilities under implementation and thus might require different skills and competencies.

In view of this, it might be necessary to develop new, operational teams. In addition to this, implementation activity is often more resource intensive than operation, so it is likely that implementation teams will need shrinking down to match the input required.

When selecting operational teams it is important to involve individuals who are close to the operation of the system. While this was desirable in earlier teams to an extent, it may not have suited competence requirements at that stage, but now it is important to bring these people to the centre of the EPE system management.

3.7.2 Identifying operational requirements and targets

The principal outputs from this stage will be:

O   The establishment of operational timescales and targets

O   The identification of operational resource requirements

O   An assessment of resource and timescale variations from outline plans agreed (see sections 2.3.4 and 3.4.2)

O   The identification of systems operators

O   The identification of additional training and support

O   The development of a reporting schedule

O   The development of a system review schedule

O   The development of a structured system maintenance schedule

O   The identification of opportunities and threats facing the EPE system.

Some of the stages identified under this section are very similar to those covered in section 3.6.2, and as such it has been decided to reference the relevant section rather than repeat the guidance given. Additional guidance will be provided where notable differences in the approach exist.

3.7.2.1 Establishing operational timescales and targets

Operational timescales will tend to focus upon routine activities, and can be built into procedures and practices if not already done. Targets are likely to be less numerous than those identified for implementation given fewer activities and the less-critical nature of the task and reduced level of supervision required. Operational targets might need to be different from implementation targets as well. Having said this, the guidance provided under section 3.6.2.1 might well prove useful at this stage.

The use of indicators applies equally in the tracking of the EPE system's performance in normal operation as it does for the implementation stage. Indeed, if established thoughtfully, and maintained, it can reduce the management effort required, through the ability to flag up potential issues and problems, and identify root causes.

3.7.2.2 Identification of operational resource requirements

The level of detail at this stage will probably be less than for the implementation plans. However, you might find the guidance given under sections 3.6.2.2 and 2.3.3.1 worth reviewing at this stage. Resource requirements are likely to centre on recurring costs more than at implementation, but it is important not to overlook one-off costs – for example, when replacement equipment is needed, new staff are taken on or improvements to existing systems are planned.

Once some experience of EPE operation has been gained it is possible that more-efficient methods and techniques will be discovered and adopted. Given this, it might be feasible to plan in savings on resource requirements looking ahead. Similarly, however, you should consider price increases in areas such as consultancy, training, salaries, equipment and communications. It is possible that some efficiencies can be realised through greater integration with other performance-evaluation processes in the organisation than was possible at implementation.

3.7.2.3 Assessment of resource and timescale variations

In addition to the other points raised under implementation planning, you should consider making notes to justify the rationale where cost savings or increases are predicted in operational plan resource requirements, in the same way as for the implementation planning (see section 3.6.2.3).

3.7.2.4 Identification of systems operators, additional training and support

Individuals or groups responsible for the ongoing operation of the EPE system may vary from those involved in the implementation. The implementation plan may well have identified this and put in place the necessary training and support for the transition. But if not, systems operators should be identified now and plans for their training and familiarisation made. As with previous sections, a training-needs analysis will prove useful in identifying the needs of new systems operators, and of existing ones if procedures and practices are amended from the implementation versions.

3.7.2.5 Development of a reporting schedule

Reporting is a key component of the ISO14031 EPE model, and thus should have been built into the implementation plan and identified as a recurring activity. However, it is possible that some reporting tasks will not be undertaken until some history of information is available or the reliability of data has been demonstrated.

All reporting activities should be scheduled to occur at intervals which ensure that the information being reported is relevant and manageable for the target audience. In addition to this, reporting at different levels should be scheduled to complement each other, and the timescales established from collection of data through to reporting should be realistic.

3.7.2.6 Development of a system review schedule

Review of the EPE system is another key element of an ISO14031 EPE system, as will be covered in section 5. In view of this it will necessary to develop a review schedule as part of the operational plan.

Reviews are most commonly conducted as meetings, but this is not necessarily required if good communications exist in the organisation and/or other forums can be used for the purpose. Whichever way, the reviews will have an output in the form of required actions to rectify problems or enhance existing systems or performance. This output should be regular and may well feed into a reporting mechanism, so it will need to be scheduled.

3.7.2.7 Development of a structured system maintenance schedule

A schedule of system maintenance will cover the routine focus on elements of the EPE system in order to ensure that the practices and procedures are being adhered to and that the system is functioning as intended. Maintenance may involve procedural or systems audits, the revision of procedures and update of instructions, or the provision of refresher training. Other activities which could be included on this schedule, although they could be scheduled independently, are calibration checks, equipment servicing and data-verification audits.

3.7.2.8 Identification of opportunities and threats facing the EPE system

The operational plan should identify foreseen opportunities or threats resulting from changes to the organisation, external influences or internal factors. Where these could have a significant effect upon the operation of the system, predicted scenarios for timescales, resource requirements and potential benefits of the system should be provided.

3.7.3 Scheduling and preparing plans, and communications

> The principal outputs from this stage will be:
>
> ○ The preparation of the operational plan
>
> ○ The identification of the management representatives and groups whose commitment will be required
>
> ○ The development of a schedule to present to the management parties identifed
>
> ○ The preparation of presentations and communications which will support the gaining of final approval and commitment from the necessary levels.

This section will follow very closely the process adopted in sections 3.6.3.2 and 3.3.5, and in view of this will not repeat details that apply equally to both situations. Instead, the stages outlined in this section will only highlight additional considerations or factors which differ. It might be useful to re familiarise yourself with sections 3.6.3.2 and 3.3.5 before continuing with this section.

3.7.3.1 The preparation of the operational plan

The operational plan can be less detailed than the implementation plan in view of the fact that changes are probable as a result of experiences in implementation.

3.7.3.2 Identification of the key management representatives and groups

The most important management groups and individuals within the organisation should have been identified already when securing commitment at earlier stages. This could form the basis of the identification of those management representatives and groups from whom you will need to secure final approval and commitment for the implementation of the EPE project. By this stage, however, the project will have become more established and implementation will be more far reaching than previous stages of the project. Some of the parties whose approval will be required may have changed, and new individuals and groups will probably need adding in.

3.7.3.3 Development of a schedule to present to the management parties identified

Be aware when developing a schedule that greater time might need to be allowed than at earlier stages of commitment gaining, given the detailed nature of the plans being presented and the consequences across the organisation of implementing ill-conceived plans.

3.7.3.4 Preparation of presentations and communications

The areas to be addressed identified in section 3.3.5.3, will still be applicable to some audiences, if not all, but the emphasis should be placed more firmly on the detail of the implementation and operational plans, and the implications for the audience.

Section 3.7 checklist

Before you embark on the next stages of EPE implementation you should have:

O   Identified the person with overall responsibility for the ongoing operation of the EPE system (system owner)

O   Identified recurring and new activities

O   Established operational responsibilities, teams, timescales and targets, and resource requirements

O   Assessed resource and timescale variations from project plans agreed

O   Identified systems operators, and additional training and support

O   Developed a schedule for reporting, system review and system maintenance

O   Identified opportunites and threats facing the EPE system

O   Prepared the operational plan

O   Identified the management representatives and groups whose approval and commitment will be required

O   Developed a schedule to present to the management parties identified

O   Prepared presentations and communications which will support the gaining of final approval and commitment from the necessary levels.

Task Heading	**Gaining final approval and commitment**
Section Reference	**3.8**
Duration	1 man day +
Difficulty Rating	2
Aims & Objectives	The aim of this section is to provide guidance on how to gain final approval for the project plans, and commitment from all key management representatives and groups to proceed to implementation.
	By following the stages of this section it is intended that you will gain approval and real management commitment, or have identified required revisions for the plans.
	The guidance provided is based on common practice and experience, but it is important to note that each individual case is likely to be different and your own knowledge of the personalities and issues involved will need to be brought into play when developing your approach.
Outputs	The principal outputs of this section will be:
	• Presentation to and/or communication with key management representatives and groups
	• Feedback from key management representatives and groups
	• Evaluation of the level of commitment secured
	• A plan of required activity to ensure that real commitment is secured
	• Identification of further barriers to EPE system development
	• Revision of plans (if required)
	• Agreement on the plan, resource requirements, timescales and milestones
	• Acknowledgement and utilisation of approval gained and commitment secured
	• List of commitments made and/or conditions agreed.
Resources Considerations	
People	Project manager
	Project team
	Top management
	Key management representatives and groups
	Advisers or consultants
Physical	Work station and office facilities
	Meeting facilities
	Access to presentation and/or communications equipment and media
	Transport
Outputs from Previous Tasks	The schedule for presenting or communicating. Section 3.7.3.3
	Presentation and support material. Section 3.7.3.4
	The implementation and operational plan reports. Sections 3.6.3 and 3.7.3
	Agreed outline of resource requirements, timescales and milestones. Section 3.4.2.
Potential Problems	• Lack of presentation competencies
	• Hidden agendas and political infighting
	• Restricted availability of key managers
	• Weak, inconsistent or unclear presentation
	• Timings of presentations.

Potential Opportunities	• Establish the value of the project • Gain strong commitment and build relationships with key players • Credibility for the project and team • Raise awareness and build understanding • Change preconceptions of key players • Obtain valuable feedback and input.

It is possible that commitment secured in section 3.4 was for the whole project, but in most cases real commitment, and resource allocation to the project, will only be forthcoming on approval of final, more-detailed implementation and operational plans. Even when whole project commitment has been gained at an early stage, it is prudent to keep key parties informed of plans as they develop. Given that the proposals presented at stage 3.4 would not have contained any of the practical considerations of the project, timescales and budgets are likely to need amending, and these will be prime areas for concern among management groups.

This section will follow very closely the process adopted in section 3.4, and in view of this will not repeat details that apply equally to both situations. Instead, the stages outlined in this section will highlight only additional considerations, or factors which differ. It might be useful to re-familiarise yourself with section 3.4 before continuing with this section.

3.8.1 Presenting, reviewing feedback, and gaining agreement

> The principal outputs from this stage will be:
>
> O The presentation of plans to key management representatives and groups, as identified
>
> O The receipt of feedback from key management representatives and groups
>
> O The evaluation of the level of real commitment secured
>
> O The identification of further actions required to secure real commitment from all key management representatives and groups
>
> O The identification of additional barriers and opportunities
>
> O The revision of plans as a result of input, feedback, conditions and commitments
>
> O Gaining agreement on the revised project plans from the key management representatives and groups
>
> O Acknowledging and utilising commitment given
>
> O Recording the details of any commitments made or conditions agreed.

3.8.1.1 Presenting and communicating

Key management representatives and groups will be aware of the project from previous presentations and work conducted on selecting indicators and preparing plans. In view of this, presentations and communications can assume a level of understanding of the basic principles of ISO14031.

The focus of the presentations should be the tangible benefits that will be derived from the project, and the implications of the project at different levels of the organisation. While commitment might exist for the benefits that will be delivered, you also need to secure commitment for the provision of the resources, time, effort and willingness to change which will be required.

At this stage you are looking for commitment to implement the EPE system as an ongoing feature of environmental management in the organisation.

3.8.1.2 Obtaining feedback

Feedback at this stage is probably more important than at any other so far. If open and honest feedback is not obtained at this stage, more problems are likely to arise when you start to implement the EPE system.

At this stage, you will have far greater flexibility to change things, and communicating changes will be easier and less damaging to the credibility of the project. If issues are not identified and they subsequently need addressing in implementation, this can have a very disruptive effect on the whole process, creating extra work and eating into resource and time allocations. Most importantly, the image of the project needs to be maintained as competent, efficient, effective and value adding. Major changes in mid-process, delays, missed deadlines and overspent budgets will serve only to erode confidence, commitment and the integrity of the project teams and management.

Apart from problems arising as a result of limited or poor feedback, also be aware that also opportunities may be missed. For instance, your proposals may require equipment, skills, facilities, materials or procedures that can be provided from sources not identified in preparatory work.

3.8.1.3 Evaluating commitment

As touched upon in the previous stage (3.8.1.2), real commitment is crucial at this stage. Therefore, identifying the level of commitment secured with different parties is another critical step in the process at this stage of the project.

3.8.1.4 Securing further commitment

Securing further commitment may well be a more immediate requirement at this stage of the project. Assess the impact of any perceived lack of commitment, and also identify opportunities to utilise strongly committed individuals or groups.

3.8.1.5 Identifying additional barriers and opportunities

The objective identification of previously unrecognised barriers to implementation will be very important at this stage of the process, so as to give the project implementation the best chance of success. Potential new opportunities which might facilitate the project should also be identified where possible.

3.8.1.6 Revision of project plans

The revision of project plans at this stage is likely to be far more involved than at the stage described in section 3.4.1.6, given that plans will have been produced in far greater detail and there will be more facets and implications to consider when changes are made. Ensure that you build in sufficient time to make any revisions required.

3.8.1.7 Agreeing the implementation and operational plans

At this stage, agreement to implementation and operational plans needs to be secured over every detail. Remember that you are agreeing more-detailed plans at this stage than at any previous stage, and thus the process is likely to be more protracted. Having said this, where plans have been developed in consideration of representations from all the key parties, and progress reports have been provided, it is possible that this stage will be little more than fine tuning or a rubber-stamping exercise.

3.8.1.8 Acknowledging and utilising commitment given

The emphasis at this stage should be placed on utilising commitment given, since you will want to get the project under way, and so too will those who have committed themselves to it.

3.8.1.9 Recording commitments and conditions

This becomes very important at this stage because the number of people involved in the project is likely to increase, and changes to personnel between implementation and operation is more likely than at any other stage in the process. The people who will have responsibility for the ongoing system, will need to know what commitments and conditions they are bound by.

Section 3.8 checklist

Before you embark on the EPE system implementation you should have:

O   Presented plans to key management representatives and groups, as identified

O   Revised plans as a result of input, feedback, conditions and commitments

O   Gained agreement on the revised project plans from the key management representatives and groups

O   Acknowledged commitment given and established means by which to utilise this commitment

O   Recorded the details of any commitments made or conditions agreed.

If you are uncertain of any aspect of your planning for the EPE system implementation, take time to review your actions (using this guidebook as reference) before proceeding to the implementation, the 'Do' phase.

Chapter 4 Do: Using Data and Information

At the end of this chapter you should have covered and understood the main requirements for implementing and operating a successful EPE system.

By following the tasks outlined, you will have implemented and be operating an EPE system (based on your plans, see section 3).

The principal outputs from this chapter will be:

- The arrangement of schedules, and preparation, for the implementation of the 'initiation' plan
- The implementation of the initiation plan, with emphasis on gaining support and commitment from all parties involved
- The establishment of data-collection processes and systems
- The establishment of data communication, handling and storage processes and systems
- The establishment of processes or systems for analysing and converting data
- The establishment of processes or systems for assessing and verifying data quality
- The development of reporting methods
- The reporting, communication and presentation of information to key interested parties.

Task Heading	**Preparing for implementation**
Section Reference	**4.1**
Duration	1 man day +
Difficulty Rating	2
Aims & Objectives	The aim of this section is to ensure that adequate preparations have been made for the 'initiation' of the EPE system implementation project. By following each stage of this section you should have identified and actioned all of the preparatory requirements identified in the initiation plan.
Outputs	The principal outputs of this section will be: • To have reviewed the initiation plan and made amendments • Identification of all parties involved in the implementation • Identification of facilities, resources and support for the initiation plan • A schedule of 'initiation' activity • To have made arrangements for communications, or training to be delivered • To have communicated the schedule of activities to all relevant parties • To have made provision for feedback from parties involved, and additional support where necessary.

Resources Considerations

People	Project manager/EPE system owner Project implementation team EPE system operators Top management Functional management Operational management Supervisory staff Operational and support staff Advisers and consultants
Physical	Work station and office facilities Meeting and training facilities Availability of information Communications networks Measuring, monitoring and test equipment and procedures Data collation, handling, storage, tools Access to presentation materials, equipment and media.
Outputs from Previous Tasks	Final approval and management commitment. Section 3.8 Project initiation plan. Section 3.6.3.1 The implementation plan. Section 3.6.3 Agreed plan of required resources, timescales and milestones. Section 3.8.1.7
Potential Problems	• Lack of real commitment at key management levels • Lack of competencies available to the project team • Weak communications • Poor relationships with key parties

	• Lack of commitment and buy-in from parties involved
	• Lack of availability of key parties
	• Lack of availability of facilities and/or support providers
	• Lack of clear, understandable processes and procedures.
Potential Opportunities	• Complementing training and development plans and initiatives
	• Reinforcing existing procedures and systems
	• Building relationships
	• Building credibility and confidence in the project and processes
	• Ability to present facts and dispel misconceptions
	• Motivation of individuals or groups through widespread involvement
	• Beginning culture change.

4.1.1 Reviewing the initiation plan

> The principal outputs from this stage will be:
>
> O   The review and amendment of the initiation plan, as required, following any commitments made or conditions agreed in gaining final approval and commitment for the implementation of the EPE system
>
> O   The identification of parties who will be involved in the initiation plan
>
> O   The identification of facilities, resources, materials and support for the initiation plan.

4.1.1.1 Revision and amendment of the initiation plan

At this stage it will be advisable to review the initiation plan developed as part of the implementation plan, to ensure that it meets the requirements of the project. This initiation plan will set the tone for the entire implementation. Thus, it is very important that it runs smoothly and delivers the necessary messages and information to enable key parties to undertake the implementation and operation of the EPE system.

The extent of any revision or amendment of the initiation plan will depend largely upon the commitments made and/or conditions agreed in order to gain final approval and commitment to the project. In addition to this, however, it is possible that you will have recognised further requirements which need incorporating into the plan, and/or areas which need changing or deleting. If you are changing or taking elements out of the plan, make sure that this will not compromise your position with any of the parties from whom commitment and approval were gained. Similarly, in adding elements to the plan, ensure that any additional resource requirements can be accommodated.

4.1.1.2 Identifying parties to be involved

The original initiation plan developed should have identified some of the key parties or positions that will be involved in the process. However, circumstances and individuals, if not the plan itself, may have changed in the interim period or as part of gaining approval and commitment.

At this stage you will need to identify, as accurately as possible, the individuals and groups, in addition to the identified members of the implementation team, who will need to be scheduled into the initiation plan activity. Figure 40 presents some examples of parties who might be involved. The indicator-set mapping work carried out in section 3.5 might also assist you in this task.

Figure 40 **Examples of parties who might be involved in the initiation plan**

Project manager	Senior management
The EPE implementation team	Operational managers
Trainers	Supervisors
Consultants or advisers	Operators
Presentation support	Administrative staff
Administrational support	Accounts
Facilities management	Training department
Public relations	Communications and IT departments
Human resources	Sales and marketing staff

Scheduling and making arrangements will require information on individuals and groups, so identification at this stage will save delays later. Included in this identification of individuals and groups should be some indication of who will fill the key roles in the project and/or ongoing operation of the EPE system. This will allow you to identify the most important parties, in order to ensure they are scheduled in, and that they have received and understood the training, and to target additional support at.

The initiation plan should incorporate a chart showing each activity in a time frame. It might prove useful to develop a record of each activity, the proposed timing and the individuals and groups required to attend. Appendix 20 provides a template which you can use to record this information. In addition the template also includes space for the actual date the activity was completed and an attendee signature to be attained (as appropriate). Further detail might be useful and/or required under training-record procedures already in existence, such as department, position, employee number and employment status.

4.1.1.3 Identifying the nature of communications, presentations, and training

Again, these areas should have been outlined in the initiation plan, but a more detailed assessment will be required at this stage. The 'notes' column in Appendix 20 provides space to identify the nature of the activity, such as mail shot, two-day training session or power-point presentation. It will be helpful to identify the duration of the activity and location to assist scheduling, though other factors such as cost and the maximum and minimum numbers of delegates permitted may also be relevant.

It will also be important to identify where specialist facilities, equipment, materials or support will be required, and the availability and lead-time for these. For example, if you are planning on using posters to raise awareness, what is the lead-time on designing and printing these, or, if you need to use an external trainer, what will be his availability? If this is not done before you come to schedule in activities, there is a greater chance that delays will occur which might affect the overall project plan.

4.1.2 Scheduling and arranging the initiation plan

The principal outputs from this section will be:

○ The development of a schedule of events for the initiation of the EPE system implementation project

○ The arrangement of communications, presentations and training delivery to each individual or group identified

○ The arrangement of necessary facilities and support

○ The provision of adequate feedback mechanisms.

There may be specialists within your organisation who can assist you with this stage. In some cases it will be required to conduct training and communications activities through, or in close conjunction with, specialist functions such as human resources, training, facilities management or site services.

4.1.2.1 Developing a schedule for the initiation plan

Having identified the individuals and groups who will be involved, and the nature of the activities, in the project initiation programme, the next task will be to schedule all of the activities. It will be necessary to identify the availability of the key individuals and groups identified, in order to accommodate requirements of the plan and the individuals.

This schedule should be consistent with the outlined timescales from the project implementation plan as agreed. The scheduling of activities should highlight any issues with planned timescales. It may be necessary to review the overall project plan timescales, if estimates for completing the initiation plan were optimistic, or where scheduling problems have arisen.

Section 3.3.5.2 identifies a number of tips for scheduling presentations, and these apply similarly to this stage of scheduling. At the initiation stage, the scheduling is likely to be more complex than for presenting to senior management, so some compromises may have to be decided upon.

Appendix 21 presents a template that you could use to schedule the activities of the initiation plan.

4.1.2.2 Arranging the delivery of the initiation plan

Arranging the delivery of the initiation plan should follow the schedule developed. You will need to consider the lead-time and availability of facilities, equipment, materials and support (as identified under stage 4.1.1.3) when making arrangements, as these may affect your ability to meet the schedule. Note that any changes made to the schedule could require changes for a large number of people, and create a cascade effect through the rest of the schedule.

4.1.2.3 Communicating the initiation activity schedule

Once the schedule and arrangements are in place for the delivery of the activities under the initiation plan, it will be necessary to communicate this to all individuals, their managers or supervisors, and any other parties who could be affected by the programme (e.g. human resources, planning, facilities management).

Communications should include details of the activity, timings, venue and any requirements of the attendee. In addition to this, the communications might include some background information, or pre-brief, and possibly a requirement to prepare for the session.

Depending on the timescale of the initiation plan, it may not be possible (or advisable) to communicate the whole schedule at once, as activities may not have all been arranged, and unforeseen events can force changes. Note that changes to the schedule once it has been communicated can be very time consuming and complex to manage well, and commonly lead to confusion and disillusionment among attendees.

Providing for feedback

It will be important to provide a mechanism by which attendees can give feedback on the effectiveness, relevance and completeness of the communications, presentations and training delivered. Figure 41 provides some examples of feedback mechanisms which you might consider applying.

Figure 41 **Examples of feedback mechanisms**

Delegate response sheet at sessions	Electronic discussion groups
Questionnaires sent to delegates after event	Project feedback telephone number or e-mail address
Telephone follow-up	Regular project feedback forums
On job follow-up assessment or audit	Suggestion boxes
One to one interviews	Representation through review-meeting structure

This feedback will give you a feel for how well-prepared individuals and groups feel they are for undertaking the implementation of the EPE system, and highlight requirements for further activity and support provision. It is possible that your organisation already has standard feedback forms for such activity, in which case you will need to check that these ask the questions which you are interested in.

Feedback mechanisms which extend beyond the activity itself can help to provide reassurance to individuals, as well as providing ongoing input for the project (this will be particularly useful at the review stage, see chapter 5). Any feedback mechanism should provide for two-way communication, as it is likely that questions will be asked through feedback or that responses are expected to issues raised.

Feedback mechanisms should be designed to obtain information as soon as possible after the event, as this is generally when the best information is given. In addition, it is common to make feedback anonymous, to encourage open and honest responses. This will very much depend upon the culture of your organisation. However, it can be useful to obtain feedback from named sources (exclusively or as well), as this can provide some good supportive material for presentations, reporting and providing rationale.

Case example   Tarmac Quarry Products Ltd: developing the EPE system through active encouragement of feedback

Tarmac Quarry Products (now part of the Anglo-American Group) operates a variety of aggregate and mineral extraction sites in the UK.

Tarmac Quarry Products Ltd is part of a business in which the development of environmental performance indicators is seen as a priority.

The consistency and completeness of the information provided by the EPE system have increased over three years. This development of the EPE system has benefited from feedback from site managers and others. The views of key stakeholders have been taken into account in the development of environmental parameters, with the need to report on resource use in relation to energy and CO_2 emissions being linked to government reporting requirements.

Section 4.1 checklist

Before you embark on the next stages of EPE implementation you should have:

O   Reviewed and amended the initiation plan, as required

O   Identified parties who will be involved in the initiation plan

O   Identified facilities, resources, materials and support for the initiation plan

O   Developed of a schedule of events for the initiation plan

O   Arranged communications, presentations and training delivery

O   Arranged necessary facilities and support

O   Provided adequate feedback mechanisms.

Task Heading	**Implementing the initiation plan**
Section Reference	**4.2**
Duration	5 man days +
Difficulty Rating	4
Aims & Objectives	The aim of this section is to ensure that the initiation plan is actioned and that any additional requirements are addressed which will affect the full implementation and/or operation of the EPE system. By following each stage of this section you will have provided all parties involved in the implementation of the EPE system with sufficient information, knowledge and skills to carry out their roles effectively.
Outputs	The principal outputs from this section will be: • To have conducted all communications, presentations and training • To have collated and assessed feedback from the parties involved as to the effectiveness of the 'initiation', the provision of resources and the level of additional support required • To have identified, prioritised and planned (if not actioned) any further activity, support or resource provision required.
Resources Considerations 　*People*	Project manager/EPE system owner Project implementation team EPE system operators Top management Functional management Operational management Supervisory staff Operational and support staff Advisers and consultants
Physical	Work station and office facilities Meeting and training facilities Availability of information Measuring, monitoring and test equipment and procedures Data collation, handling, storage and management tools and procedures Access to analysis tools and statistical packages.
Outputs from Previous Tasks	Final approval and management commitment. Section 3.8 Project initiation plan. Section 3.6.3.1 Preparations for implementation. Section 4.1.2 Agreed plans for implementation and operation. Sections 3.6.3 and 3.7.3 Agreed plan of required resources, timescales and milestones. Section 3.8.1.7
Potential Problems	• Lack of real commitment at key management levels • Lack of availability and commitment of key parties • Lack of availability of facilities and/or support providers • Communications, presentations and training pitched at too high a level

	• Resistance to change
	• Lack of clear understandable processes and procedures
Potential Opportunities	• Building awareness, knowledge and understanding among interested parties
	• Ability to present facts and dispel misconceptions
	• Complementing training and development plans and initiatives
	• Reinforcing existing procedures and systems
	• Building credibility and confidence in the project and processes
	• Motivation of individuals or groups.

4.2.1 Conducting initiation plan activites

The principal outputs from this section will be:

O   Delivering the activities identified under the initiation plan

O   The collation and assessment of feedback

O   The identification and planning of additional requirements.

4.2.1.1 Delivering the activities

The delivery of the activities planned and scheduled under the initiation plan will require a degree of monitoring, and it will be worth keeping some record of each activity session and the individuals involved (where existing training and communications procedures do not require this).

Some key points to look at when monitoring the delivery of activities are listed below.

* Was the activity conducted according to the schedule timings?
* Was the activity delivered effectively?
* Did the activity fulfil its intended purpose? (From feedback and observation)
* What improvements (if any) could be made to the activity content to enhance the message?
* How many identified individuals were not covered under the activity?
* Were any of the individuals not covered key to the project?
* Were individuals not covered in their scheduled activity covered at another time?
* Were the facilities, equipment and materials used suitable for the activity?
* Were the media used suitable?
* Were the timings of the activity suitable?

There are likely to be other areas of the activity delivery that you will want to monitor as well indeed, your organisation may have a standard evaluation approach. It is important that the project manager and members of the team are visible during the activity, gathering informal (as well as formal) feedback, observing and providing support. Constant monitoring of these activities is important, particularly in large-scale projects, so that problems can be addressed quickly and are not allowed to run throughout the 'initiation' schedule.

This process of monitoring the activities will also provide you with a valuable feel for the morale of individuals and groups within and outside the project, and help in the identification of any unforeseen opportunities and threats at an early stage. It will also provide valuable experience when planning and implementing further activities and initiatives.

4.2.1.2 Collation and assessment of feedback

In the previous step we talked about monitoring the delivery of activities and collating informal and formal feedback from individuals and groups. This is a very important part of the activity delivery, as it will provide indications of weaknesses and strengths in the approaches taken, and help you identify improvements and requirements for further activity.

Feedback is generally of higher quality the sooner it is obtained. With this in mind the feedback mechanism should be available at the activity delivery point, and efforts should be made to obtain feedback at this point. This might involve building in an extra ten or fifteen minutes at the end of the session, and physically collecting feedback forms (for example).

Once feedback has been obtained, it is good practice to collate this, analyse and review it. Again this is best done as soon after the activity and receipt of feedback as possible, involving as many people from the delivery team as possible. 'Wash up' meetings, conducted immediately after the delivery of an activity, are a common means of achieving this.

Remote and passive communications and training by their nature do not allow for this level of feedback collation and analysis, but it is still worth making the effort to get feedback as soon as possible, be it from deliverers, or more importantly from the target audience themselves.

You may not agree with all the feedback obtained, and indeed you will need to assess whether there are underlying motives behind some responses, but such feedback can indicate the level of motivation, commitment and interest in the project and subject. This will be useful for identifying barriers and opportunities for the project, and developing plans to address these.

Appendix 22 provides a template for the recording of the output from this collation and assessment, including space to identify additional activity requirements (as covered in the next section).

4.2.1.3 Identification and planning of additional requirements

The collation and assessment of feedback, combined with observations and experiences, will provide information from which to identify further activity requirements. This might take the form of additional training, refresher training, more communications and presentations or the provision of information and support, to name but some of the most common.

As mentioned throughout the planning phase, resource and time availability may not be good, and this is likely to limit the amount of additional activity that can be undertaken. With this in mind, it will be necessary to prioritise the additional activities identified, and assess if any are fundamental to the success of the project, and/or could be addressed in a different, resource- and time-effective manner.

Where additional activities are not possible in the short term, interim solutions may be found, with further activity identified for the future when resources and time will be available. Deferred activities should be highlighted in the review phase of the EPE system.

Details of further action identified can be entered onto the template of Appendix 22.

Section 4.2 checklist

Before you embark on the next stages of EPE implementation you should have:

O   Delivered the activities identified under the initiation plan

O   Collated and assessed feedback obtained

O   Identified and planned additional activities as required.

Task Heading	**Establishing data collection**
Section Reference	**4.3**
Duration	5 man days +
Difficulty Rating	3
Aims & Objectives	The aim of this section is to establish efficient and effective data-collection practices, in line with the implementation and operational plans developed. By following each stage of this section you will have developed an operational data-collection system to support the stated needs of EPE system and your organisation.
Outputs	The principal outputs from this section will be: • The provision and application of any monitoring or measuring equipment or methodology for the collection of data as required • The implementation of procedures and practices for the collection of data • An initial check-back assessment for data collectors • The provision of any support or instruction required by parties involved in the collection of data.
Resources Considerations People	Project manager/EPE system owner Project implementation team EPE system operators Functional and operational management Supervisory staff Operational and support staff Advisers and consultants
Physical	Work station and office facilities Meeting and training facilities Availability of information Transport Communications networks Measuring, monitoring and test equipment and procedures.
Outputs from Previous Tasks	Final approval and management commitment. Section 3.8 The implementation and operational plans. Sections 3.6.3 and 3.7.3 Plans for further activity, support or resource provision identified at 'initiation'. Section 4.2.1.3
Potential Problems	• Lack of real commitment at key management levels • Lack of competencies available to the project team • Poor relationships with parties involved • Lack of real understanding of requirements • Lack of commitment and buy-in by parties involved • Resistance to change and new ways of working • Lack of clear understandable processes and procedures • Lack of guidance and support • Lack of measuring and monitoring equipment and procedures

Potential Opportunities	• Building awareness, knowledge and understanding among interested parties • Motivation of individuals or groups through widespread involvement • Complementing or enhancing existing data-collection processes • Building relationships • Building credibility and confidence in the project and processes • Beginning culture change.

4.3.1 Provision of equipment, practices and procedures

The principal outputs from this stage will be:

O   The provision of equipment and methods by which data will be recorded

O   The implementation of procedures and practices for the collection of data

O   The checking back on data collection

O   The provision of additional support and instruction.

4.3.1.1 Provision of equipment and methods

The identification of required actions within the agreed implementation (and/or operational) plan should have detailed any equipment require ments for the measuring and recording of data for indicators. This equipment will include not only measuring and monitoring equipment, but also equipment for the recording, handling, conversion, storage and communication of data. Therefore equipment might be a stack-emissions monitor, or a desktop computer for recording and communicating any data collected.

How specialist the equipment required is will probably affect the lead-time on obtaining, installing and commissioning it. Further consideration, relating to the operations of the organisation, or the release of resources, may further affect the timescales for having equipment operational.

The use of equipment will probably be subject to a predetermined methodology, stipulated either by the suppliers/manufacturers or by the project manager and team. Where equipment was not available for practical training at the initiation stage, it is probable that further training will be required. Similarly, if a considerable lead-time to getting equipment operational has been experienced, some refresher training might be necessary.

Where data-collection equipment is already in operation, it might be necessary to ensure that sufficiently trained operators exist to use the equipment.

This will be particularly important if new data is to be collected or different terms of expression used. The actual methods of use for existing equipment are also worth checking, as long-established practices can often deviate from methodology needed to meet data-quality requirements.

With most equipment used for measuring there will be a need for calibration checks to be carried out on a regular basis, as deemed suitable for the equipment in question. Equipment suppliers will usually be able to advise on the appropriate intervals. Calibration checks are important for EPE, as reliable and consistent data will be required if the best information is to be available at the reporting, review and decision-making stages.

If your organisation already operates quality-management systems and/or a formal EMS, it is likely that calibration procedures are already in place, but it is worth checking that these are actually being complied with, and that the tolerances and frequencies are suitable for your requirements. Note that equipment being used for monitoring areas covered by legislation needs to comply with any requirements stipulated therein.

4.3.1.2 Implementation of procedures and practices

From the indicators developed, it is probable that not all data will be collected and recorded with the use of equipment. Observations, inspections, audits, interviews and the examination of documents and records can all be sources of data. The implementation plan should have identified and developed required practices and procedures along with equipment, as part of the detail of actions, and this should form the basis for the work in this stage.

Case Example   Unique Images, Bradford: collecting data on production waste

Unique Images is a wholly owned subsidiary of Hallmark Inc. and provides bespoke design and manufacture of greetings cards and giftware to major multiple retailers in the UK.

Unique Images has implemented a thorough system for the segregation and measurement of production waste across all of its manufacturing operations. Green teams were established through all departments to develop and train in procedures for the correct identification, segregation and measurement for each waste stream.

Segregated waste is taken to specified reception points, where the operator will key his personal identification number, the departmental code and confirm the waste type. The waste is then weighed before being sent to the compactor. All of the information keyed, including the weight of material data, is then automati-

---

cally transferred to a data base which is accessible by the environmental management team for analysis and production of waste reporting information.

Progress against waste minimisation goals can be accurately tracked through this system, and the level of detail provided can help the environmental management team quickly identify where problems are occurring.

The full capital costs of the project were covered by the revenues from segregated waste within 18 months, despite dramatic reductions in the commodity prices for the waste being generated.

New procedures and practices may well have been communicated and training conducted as part of the initiation plan. If not, this will need to take place before they can be implemented. Feedback should be obtained on new procedures and practices at this stage. In addition to this, existing procedures and practices will need checking to ensure that they are being applied correctly.

Procedures should be:

* Relevant
* Clear and understandable
* Manageable
* Practical for the conditions under which they may be required for use
* Able to produce data of a reliable and consistent nature routinely.

New procedures and practices can meet with resistance. However, if the procedures developed apply the principles outlined above, then this should reduce any resistance to their implementation. The use of flow charts can prove effective for clear presentation and aiding understanding (see section 3.6.1.5).

Developing new procedures will require an evaluation of the following key points:

* Data required
* The tolerance on data accuracy which is acceptable
* The means of data collection
* The individual or group responsible for collecting the data
* The frequency of data collection
* The timings of data collection
* The conditions under which data are collected
* Any foreseeable circumstances which might affect data collection, e.g. shut-down periods, severe weather conditions, holiday or break periods.

Following this process may well identify improvements that can be made to existing procedures and practices. These can then be fed through the review phase of the EPE system.

In collecting data, any anomalies in the data or influential factors identified should be recorded and kept with the data through to the analysis stage, and beyond if necessary.

4.3.1.3 Checking back on data collection

Once procedures, practices and equipment are in place and operational, it would be advisable to check back on the data-collection process to ensure that data are being collected in line with project intentions. In addition to this, the check provides an opportunity for the implementation team to identify any operational difficulties that will need addressing, and requirements for support. In addition to the more functional nature of the check back, it also provides an opportunity for building relationships with the data collectors and communicators (where data collection and communication require a human input).

It is recommended that check backs are scheduled for all key data-collection activities, with possibly more than one check back for very complex or critical areas. The sooner the check backs are conducted, the sooner any problems can be corrected, and the greater the level of perceived support provided by the implementation team.

The check-back process is the initial stage of an ongoing verification process, and as such similar skills and techniques will need to be applied. For further detail on this refer to section 4.5.

4.3.1.4 Providing additional support and instruction

The feedback obtained from the activities conducted under the initiation plan, feedback from the introduction of procedures and practices, and the findings of the check backs will provide information on what additional support and instruction will be required.

It should be recognised that communications, presentations, training, instruction and support are rarely truly effective if provided as a one-off. These processes need to be ongoing and flexible, so that they are responsive to needs as they arise, as well as predictive of future needs.

Failure to provide additional support and instruction at the right times can result in unreliable data input into the EPE system, and the disillusionment of data collectors and handlers. For this reason, flexibility in planning, and the provision of contingency resource, can prove very important.

Section 4.3 checklist

Before you embark on the next stages of EPE implementation you should have:

○   Provided equipment and methods by which data will be recorded

○   Implemented procedures and practices for the collection of data

○   Checked back on data collection

○   Provided additional support and instruction as required.

Task Heading	**Establishing data communication, handling and storage**
Section Reference	**4.4**
Duration	3 man days +
Difficulty Rating	2
Aims & Objectives	The aim of this section is to establish efficient and effective processes and systems for the communication of collected data, and the good handling and maintenance of that data. By following each stage of this section you will have developed processes and systems for data communication, handling and storage which are suitable to needs and resources of your organisation, efficient and effective.
Outputs	The principal outputs of this section will be: • The provision and implementation of equipment, resources, procedures and practices for communicating information • The effective and efficient communication of collected data to identified individuals, departments or data bases (if systems based) • The provision of equipment and resources for data handling and storage • The provision of any support or instruction required by parties involved in the communication, handling or storage of data.
Resources Considerations *People*	Project manager/EPE system owner Project implementation team EPE system operators Functional and operational management Supervisory staff Operational and support staff Advisers and consultants
Physical	Work station and office facilities Meeting and training facilities Availability of information Communications networks for the transfer of collected data Data handling and storage procedures, tools, facilities and/or equipment
Outputs from Previous Tasks	Final approval and management commitment. Section 3.8 The implementation and operational plans. Sections 3.6.3 and 3.7.3 Implementation of data-collection practices, procedures, equipment and methodology. Section 4.3.1 Plans for further activity, support or resource provision identified at 'initiation'. Section 4.2.1.3
Potential Problems	• Lack of real commitment at key management levels • Lack of real understanding of requirements • Lack of commitment and buy-in by parties involved • Resistance to change and new ways of working • Lack of clear, understandable processes and procedures • Lack of guidance and support.

Potential Opportunities	• Building awareness, knowledge and understanding among interested parties
	• Motivation of individuals or groups through widespread involvement
	• Complementing or enhancing existing data communication, handling and storage processes and procedures
	• Building credibility and confidence in the project and processes
	• Increasing frequency and amount of data handled by the system.

4.4.1 Communication of data

The principal outputs from this section will be:

○ The provision of data-communication mechanisms

○ The implementation of data-communication mechanisms

○ The effective and efficient communication of data.

4.4.1.1 Providing data-communication mechanisms

The implementation plan should identify the data communication mechanisms that need to be provided for each data stream. The sophistication of such mechanisms can range from electronic information transfer systems, to memos through the internal mail. It will need to be assessed whether the mechanisms identified are suitable for the task in terms of the:

• Nature of the data to be communicated
• Volume of the data to be communicated
• Operational environment
• Users of the communication mechanism
• Timescales stipulated.

It is likely that communication mechanisms will vary across the organisation, but there are often efficiencies to be realised in making the different mechanisms compatible. This is especially true for electronic data transfer systems.

You will also need to consider the lead-time for any equipment required and the effect this might have on the overall implementation schedule and plan.

4.4.1.2 The implementation of data communication mechanisms

If new data-communication mechanisms are being implemented under the project, it will be necessary to provide instruction and training for data communicators. In most cases the data collectors and/or converters will also need some understanding of the requirements of the communication mechanism in order that they prepare data in a format and timescale which is suitable.

For more simple communication mechanisms the provision of procedures will probably suffice as instruction, but more involved or technical approaches might require more formal training and support. In such cases it is possible that facilities and equipment will only be available for training operators once it has been installed, which might delay the full implementation of the systems. Further consideration needs to be given to the time it will take to bed-in more involved mechanisms, and the disruption the implementation of new systems might have on existing practices.

Communication mechanisms that are routine and automated will generally be more reliable than mechanisms that are applied irregularly and/or require a high degree of human involvement. However, many communication mechanisms will involve human input, and cost implications can prevent change to this. In such cases checks and audits can be applied to look at the efficiency and effectiveness of the communication mechanisms employed. In addition, or alternatively, indicators can be established which track performance against some key operating criteria, or monitoring systems can be established to report by exception. Some key areas to consider are shown in the following list.

- Are communications being initiated on time?
- Are communications being received on time?
- Are communications being received at the right point?
- Are the data communicated in the specified format?
- Are data being altered or distorted in transfer?
- Are the data legible on receipt?

Further considerations when assessing the effectiveness and efficiency of data communications will centre around the flow of data from point of collection, through initial conversion (if applicable), into the communication mechanism, and on to data analysis. Again the less the data are handled and converted by people the more accurate and reliable they are likely to be. Having said this, it is important to conduct checks on all data, especially automatically collected and communicated data, as there is less likelihood of errors being detected should they occur in the process of handling the data.

Ensuring effective and efficient communication at each level in the chain is important, as any weakness in the chain of communications will impact on all subsequent processes. The chain of communications will only be as strong as its weakest link.

4.4.2 Handling and storage of data

> The principal outputs from this section will be:
>
> o   The provision of data handling and storage facilities
>
> o   The Implementation of data handling and storage processes
>
> o   The effective and efficient handling and storage of data.

4.4.2.1 Provision of data handling and storage facilities

Handling and storage of data is often overlooked, yet it can form a very important part of any EPE system. From the point of collection, data can be handled by a large number of people any number of times. Handling in this context refers to the transfer or conversion of data. When data are not being handled they will need to be stored in a safe, secure and accessible manner. This applies to data that may have been subsequently converted, as these data might be required to substantiate or check information derived from them, or as the basis for alternative analysis.

In view of this it is important to provide suitable data handling and storage facilities at each level where data are handled and stored. Again facilities can be simple or sophisticated, with electronic methods generally offering the most efficient and flexible operating solutions, although possibly at a higher cost in terms of capital and maintenance.

Lead-times for the provision of data handling and storage facilities need to be considered in terms of the impact on the implementation plan. In addition, some data transfer to storage media (e.g. scanning or transfer to microfilm) can make unavailable for a short period information which could be important if the data are recent and/or in regular demand.

4.4.2.2 Implementation of data handling and storage processes

Where sophisticated approaches are adopted, training and support are more likely to be required than for more straightforward approaches such as manual, paper-based systems. Procedures will probably be able to provide sufficient instruction for simple systems, especially where these do not differ too greatly from existing practices. Indeed, it is advisable to try to adopt existing practices where suitable.

It is recommended that data handling and storage processes should have some form of tracking system in place and a routine of 'backing up' information.

Tracking points can be established at key data-transfer stages in the process, for example at submission of collected data to the office, input of data to the weekly report and despatch of the weekly report to the environmental management team. This will allow you to identify how far data have progressed through the system. The accuracy of this depends upon the regularity of tracking points. Alternatively, tracking can be done at time intervals (which could be at request), but this is very difficult to achieve with any non-electronic system, especially when data are not where they should be at a given time, which is usually when you will want the information. The system adopted should consider the cost or resource input required and weigh this up against the importance of the information it will provide.

'Backing up' data is usually associated with computerised processes, but here we use the term to mean copying data. This should be done at key stages in the process, particularly when data are leaving one area or department for another, or at specific times. The need to back up data will depend on the level of risk of loss, damage or alteration to data in handling or storage, how easy the data are to collect again, and the perceived importance of the data.

Most data-copying systems are relatively cheap, so safeguarding against risk in this way is often believed to warrant the cost. Backing up data when they are leaving an area or a department can be particularly important if the data are likely to be required there for other purposes afterwards.

As with communication mechanisms, the efficiency and effectiveness of data handling and storage systems can be monitored through checks and audits, and/or by tracking indicators of performance. More reliable systems might need only monitoring for exceptions as and when they occur. Some key points to consider when assessing the effectiveness and efficiency of data handling and storage systems might be:

- The completeness of data records
- The vulnerability of stored data to damage, alteration or loss
- The availability of data
- The speed with which data can be retrieved
- The condition of data in storage
- The timing of data at different points in the system against plan
- The amount of errors introduced through data handling at different stages
- The amount of damage to, or loss of, data occurring in handling
- The security of data when being handled.

Section 4.4 checklist

Before you embark on the next stages of EPE implementation you should have:

○ Provided data-communication mechanisms, and data handling and storage facilities

○ Implemented data communication, handling and storage processes

○ The effective and efficient communication, handling and storage of data.

Task Heading	**Establishing data conversion, analysis, assessment and verification**
Section Reference	**4.5**
Duration	5 man days +
Difficulty Rating	4
Aims & Objectives	The aim of this section is to implement procedures and processes for the conversion, analysis and assessment of data collected under the EPE system, and establish some verification process.
	By following each stage of this section you will have implemented procedures and processes necessary to allow the conversion, analysis and assessment of data in line with implementation and operational plans. In addition to this, there will be flexibility to analyse data in differing ways as deemed appropriate to the circumstances, and the verification of data and information produced from the process.
Outputs	The principal outputs of this section will be:
	• The implementation of plans to allow for accurate, consistent and prescribed conversion, analysis and assessment of data
	• Flexibility to analyse and assess data in different ways, as appropriate
	• The accurate and consistent analysis and conversion of data
	• The provision of any support or instruction required by parties involved in the conversion, analysis, assessment and verification of data
	• The identification of any suspect data, by comparison with expected norms, and verification of data and information produced
	• The production of information on the environmental performance of the organisation.
Resources Considerations	
People	Project manager/EPE system owner
	Project implementation team
	Data analysts
	Advisers and consultants
Physical	Sound data handling and storage practices
	Data handling and storage tools, facilities and/or equipment
	Statistical and analysis packages
Outputs from Previous Tasks	The effective and efficient communication, handling and storage of collected data, within agreed timescales. Section 4.4.2
	The implementation and operational plans. Section 3.6.3 and 3.7.3
	Plans for further activity, support or resource provision identified at 'initiation'. Section 4.2.3
Potential Problems	• Lack of competencies available to the project team
	• Lack of real understanding of requirements
	• Lack of clear understandable processes and procedures
	• Lack of guidance and support.

Potential Opportunities	• Building awareness, knowledge and understanding among interested parties
	• Complementing or enhancing existing data analysis and conversion processes
	• Building credibility and confidence in the project and processes
	• Identification of significant issues or opportunities for the organisation.

4.5.1 Conversion and analysis of data

> The principal outputs from this section will be:
>
> ○ The provision of facilities and equipment for the conversion and analysis of data
>
> ○ The conversion and analysis of data.

4.5.1.1 Providing for the conversion and analysis of data

Not all data will require converting prior to analysis, though it is likely that more conversion will be required the greater the amount of data that need analysing and the greater the number of levels of indicator which have been developed.

For example, if you want to know the monthly oil-consumption figure for a piece of manufacturing equipment, the monthly data collected will suffice. However, if you want to know this information for all manufacturing equipment, you will have to add the data collected for each machine, thus converting the data, albeit in a very simple manner. Similarly, if data are collected daily, then the daily figures will need adding up for the month or if you want relate the oil consumption to hours of operation, or index the usage to a base figure derived from consumption two years ago, then this will again involve data conversion.

Conversion of data is likely to occur in two stages.

• Initial conversion. Data collected require conversion so that they can be used in a specified indicator. For example, adding collected data, adjusting readings, putting data into standard units of measurement, calculation of monetary value from data.

• Indicator conversion. Data, in the form detailed by the indicator specification, are converted into information by applying the indicator. For example, data are divided by another variable to get a relative measure.

In many cases the conversion of data will not be too involved, and therefore little provision of resource equipment and facilities will be required.

However, where large amounts of data are being converted, or where the conversions are of a complex nature, then the provision of systems (electronic or manual) will probably be required. Increasingly, computers are being used for such tasks, as they offer the most efficient, accurate and flexible approaches, especially as capital costs are reducing, software is becoming more powerful and user friendly, and availability of skilled operators is increasing.

This application of computers also applies to the analysis of the information resulting from conversion through the indicators specified. Analysis can become quicker, more accurate and far more sophisticated through the use of software with analytical and statistical capability (such as spreadsheet applications). It will also prove useful for the presentation of information, which will assist reporting and communications at a later stage (see section 4.6).

Whether you choose electronic or manual approaches to data conversion and information analysis, it will be necessary to provide adequate facilities, and an adequate environment in which to conduct the work. The facilities will need to accommodate data communication, handling and storage equipment, as well as the means for conversion and analysis. Further to this, the environment should provide the analyst with time when he will not be distracted or disturbed.

4.5.1.2 Conducting the conversion and analysis of data

In the data-collection stage (section 4.3), we mentioned that it might be most appropriate for initial conversion to take place prior to communication of data to the point of analysis. This will reduce the amount of data being supplied, presenting the analysts only with the data they need.

This approach can spread the work load around the different data-collection points, and will speed up the analysis process, as well as placing less pressure on the communication mechanisms, and the handling and storage practices at the point of analysis.

The drawbacks of this approach are that:

- It limits the analysis that is possible, if data are required in a different format (e.g. consumption figures by week as opposed to month, or broken down by operator as opposed to the department)
- Requesting the data in a different format will probably add time to the process, and can also confuse and annoy the data providers
- Data converted by a wide range of parties are likely to be less reliable overall than if the conversion is conducted by a few skilled analysts (albeit that a level of data checking is removed)

- Opportunities to reduce equipment and training requirements (and associated costs) are lost.

The last point here highlights the need for training and instruction in the conversion of data and the analysis of information. As with the previous stages of this section, the extent and format of the training, instruction and subsequent support required will be dependent upon the complexity of the tasks, and the competencies of the individuals involved.

The use of computerised systems and software can reduce some of the competence requirements of operators in converting and analysis, but will probably require skills for using the equipment and software applications, which in turn might need training.

To maximise the potential of the analysis stage, it will be useful to allow the analysts some flexibility in the approach taken. While the EPE-system plans will have identified information required for reporting to interested parties and the use of the environmental management function, analysing different aspects of the data can provide valuable insights into issues, and possibly provide more interesting information than originally foreseen. The level of flexibility which you can build in will be limited by time, resource availability and the competence of the analyst. The potential value of allowing greater flexibility will depend upon the vision and skill of the analyst, and the range of relevant data available for analysis.

4.5.2 Verifying data and performance information

The principal outputs from this section will be:

- The identification of suspect data
- The establishment of verification processes for data and information
- The development of verification records
- Providing additional support and feedback.

4.5.2.1 Identifying suspect data

At the conversion and analysis stages, an important function of the data converters and analysers will be to assess roughly the data or information for its accuracy. Suspect data will generally be data that does not conform to predicted outcomes and/or previous experiences.

Sometimes it will be possible to cross check data by comparing them to other variables, such as:

- Emissions from a stack vs. manufacturing schedule
- Fuel consumption vs. planned or actual miles
- Paper used vs. toner and cartridge use
- Material sent to landfill vs. area of excavation.

Suspect data is not necessarily inaccurate, and it will be worth checking with data collectors, initial converters and people who can influence the variable being measured, to see if any abnormal occurrences should be recognised which were not reported with the data. If there is still no obvious reason for the discrepancy, then a more detailed check or verification will probably be required.

Even at this stage it should not be assumed that an error has been made, as it is possible that the data are correct and there is a serious operational problem to be addressed. Where the data stream provides information on an area of activity that has few or infrequent other checks applied or is not highly visible problems can easily go undetected.

Some examples are given below:

- Leaks in underground storage tanks or pipelines
- Gaseous emissions
- Faulty weight-checking equipment
- Poorly maintained equipment
- Store-room lights left on
- Dripping taps
- Demand-driven waste-removal contracts
- Theft of materials
- Fly tipping
- Deviations from route plans.

4.5.2.2 Establishment of verification processes for data and information

Verification processes for data and information produced by the EPE system should be established to provide some assurance that the information being used to make management decisions, and being communicated, is reliable. This will be especially important when reporting information externally, in particular to potentially hostile interested parties.

In respect of using information as a basis for decision making, it is clear that inaccurate or distorted information can lead to incorrect evaluations and assessments of situations. This could lead to unnecessary or inappropriate action being taken, or no action being taken when it is actually required.

Reporting also needs reliable information, to establish and support the credibility of environmental management activity and the organisation as a whole. If inaccurate information is reported, this may be contradicted by other evidence or more accurate data obtained in the future or through other means.

Verification processes can be established in a number of ways, the most common of which are identified below.

- Routine or scheduled, i.e. the verification of data is conducted to a predetermined schedule in a similar way to system audits
- By exception, i.e. the verification of data occurs only when data values fall outside predetermined tolerances
- In reaction, i.e. the verification of data occurs only when there is an obvious or a suspected problem or incident
- A combination of any of or all three of the above.

As the fourth approach points out, all three of the above approaches could be used in combination, and this probably will provide the most comprehensive assurance for the organisation.

In developing the verification process you should consider the resource, time and cost implications. Verifying data in reaction is likely to be the least resource intensive, yet it does little to ensure data reliability and becomes a damage-limitation exercise. Setting tolerances can prove a cost-effective option if well judged and the system is running well, but if tolerances are unsuitable problems can be missed, or an excessive amount of verification will be required. Similarly, if the system is performing badly, verification will be excessive and will not necessarily provide a systematic approach.

Scheduled verification provides a systematic approach, and if kept secret can prevent the problem of verification-day remedies being applied in the areas concerned. However, scheduled verification does potentially require more resources than are necessary, and can miss problems depending on the timing and frequency of the verifications.

Verification of data can be conducted either up the data chain (from collection to analysis) or horizontally, testing samples of data across a number of data chains at certain levels. Whichever approach is adopted, the verifier should be looking for evidence that the data have been collected, converted, handled, stored and communicated in accordance with procedures and agreed practices. Verifications should also be conducted for information produced from analysis, and the procedures and practices assessed for any weaknesses, ambiguity and unnecessary bureaucracy.

Where problems are discovered, the verification should identify and agree remedial action, with timescales, potentially affected data should be re-checked and produced again if necessary, and the impact of any errors should be assessed and decisions taken for further action.

4.5.2.3 Development of verification records

Any verification of data conducted, be it at desktop level when suspect data is first identified, or as an in-depth investigation, should be recorded. This will provide information for use at reviews to assess how well the system is working, if any additional training and support are required, what remedial action has been taken and what further action is required.

The record should also identify any relevant costs and savings resulting from the problems identified and their rectification. This information can then be used to demonstrate the benefit provided by the EPE system.

4.5.2.4 Providing additional support and feedback

As mentioned above, the analysis, verification and assessment process should allow for easier identification of problems, and highlight where additional support is required. In addition to this, where successes are identified there might be opportunity to use these as examples to support improvement in other areas.

The feedback of findings from this stage will be important for the rectification of problems, and the motivation and reward of strong performance. The reporting element of the EPE system should be designed to capture this information and convey it as appropriate for the situation and audience. However, the system could be enhanced if independent channels of communication are established which allow for feedback to be given quickly so that it can be acted upon accordingly.

4.5.3 Assessing and summarising environmental performance information

> The principal outputs from this section will be:
>
> O   The assessment of environmental performance information
>
> O   The summarisation of environmental performance information.

4.5.3.1 Assessing environmental performance information

Assessment of the information refers to the comparison of indicator information outputs with the stated goals or environmental performance criteria of the organisation. Assessment provides the link between the analysis and the environmental performance aims of the organisation, and should highlight to management areas of strong performance and areas where remedial or additional action is required. Assessment is likely to be performed by the analysts and/or environmental management, and will probably be adequately provided for by resources allocated for conversion and analysis. The outputs from the assessment of the information will feed into the reporting stage and the review processes.

4.5.3.2 Summarising environmental performance information

Having analysed, verified and assessed the environmental performance information derived from the indicators and data collected, it will be necessary to summarise this information in a format which will support the reporting of information to identified interested parties, and provide a focus for the review process.

The summary should:

* Provide detail of the information for each indicator
* Present any additional information or notes which are relevant to the indicator
* Identify the level of performance against each indicator over time
* Identify the level of performance against each indicator between comparable areas of the organisation
* Identify the level of performance shown by the indicator information against stated environmental performance criteria, goals, objectives and/or targets.

Commentary on the performance and suggested or recommended action can also be included, though this may be deemed more appropriate for the reporting and review stages.

Section 4.5 checklist

Before you embark on the next stages of EPE implementation you should have:

O   Provided facilities and equipment for the conversion, and analysis of data

O   Conducted the conversion and analysis of data

- ○   Verified data and performance information

- ○   Identified suspect data

- ○   Established verification processes for data and information

- ○   Developed verification records

- ○   Assessed and summarised environmental performance information.

Task Heading	**Reporting, presenting, and communicating information**
Section Reference	**4.6**
Duration	5 man days
Difficulty Rating	4
Aims & Objectives	The aim of this section is to establish processes and systems for the reporting, presentation and communication to interested parties of information generated from the EPE system. By following each stage of this section you will have developed a reliable and robust mechanism for reporting information to all key interested parties (as identified), internal and external to the organisation.
Outputs	The principal outputs of this section will be: • The identification of report format and content, detailing reporting dates, recipients, content, style and format (section 3.7.2.5) • The provision of feedback facilities for all interested parties • Approval to report information • The review of the original reporting schedule • The provision of resources, equipment and skills to produce to schedule consistent and reliable reports, presentations and communications • The production and dissemination of reports, presentations, and communications • The analysis of feedback received.
Resources Considerations People	Project manager/EPE system owner Project implementation team Top management Functional management Auditors and verifiers Advisers and consultants Publishers and distributors
Physical	Work station and office facilities Availability of relevant information Communication systems Data handling and storage tools, facilities and/or equipment Presentation materials, equipment and media
Outputs from Previous Tasks	The production of environmental performance information. Section 4.5.3.2 Records of information assessments and verifications. Section 4.5.2.3 The implementation and operational plans. Sections 3.6.3 and 3.7.3
Potential Problems	• Reliance on verification of data by exception only • Lack of real understanding of the needs of interested parties • Lack of honesty and objectivity • Lack of clear presentation

	• Late or irregular reporting
	• Information is irrelevant or of no interest by the time it is reported
	• Information gets into the wrong hands.
Potential Opportunities	• Building awareness, knowledge and understanding among interested parties.
	• Ability to present facts and dispel misconceptions
	• Motivation of individuals or groups
	• Building credibility, relationships, trust and confidence in project and organisation
	• Ability to communicate tangible environmental performance information to key interested parties.

4.6.1 Establishing the reporting environmental performance information

The principal outputs from this section will be:

O   The determination of the report format, content and schedule

O   Approval to report information.

4.6.1.1 Determining the report format, content and schedule

The work carried out under Section 3.6.1.3, in the implementation planning phase, backed up by the scheduling of reporting in the operational plan (see section 3.7.2.5), will provide the basis for this stage.

From the information produced through the use of the indicators selected and any additional analysis undertaken, the planned reporting approach may require altering. In addition to this, changes in resource availability or the cost of producing reports in a particular format may well necessitate changes to the original plans.

With information now available you will need to assess which elements will be beneficial and of interest to the audience, or indeed desirable to report from the organisation's point of view. Similarly the reporting schedule needs to reviewed to assess whether the timescales are realistic, and if the information produced is suited to the format of the report planned. It is possible that initial reporting formats and timings will be scaled down, but you should bear in mind any commitments made or conditions agreed when taking any such decisions.

In reviewing the reporting format and schedule, you should consider the following points:

• Will the information being reported be of interest and use to the interested parties targeted?

- Are the information and terms of expression relevant and understandable for the targeted interested parties?
- Are the reporting intervals achievable and in line with the expectations of the interested parties?
- Are the media which you will use to communicate the information going to be effective in reaching interested parties and conveying the right messages?
- Is the mode of delivery suitable for interested parties' needs?
- Is the cost of the format selected justified?
- Is the format adopted capable of delivering within specified and/or expected timescales?
- Is the format adopted capable of delivering accurately to the target audience?
- Is the format adopted capable of delivering information in the right condition?
- Does the format adopted provide for feedback or will feedback channels need to be developed?

This last point, relating to feedback, may not have been considered in the planning stages, but it is important. Feedback channels should be accessible, fast acting, two way, preferably ongoing, and in line with the competencies and culture of the audience

4.6.1.2 Gaining approval to report information

While you may well have gained approval for the EPE system implementation project at an earlier juncture, it is probable that you will need to gain from senior management approval to report the information generated. This is more likely to be the case where the recipients of the information are external to the organisation and/or where the information and issues it relates to are sensitive. It is possible that you will want to review information that is to be reported through the review process (see Chapter 5) prior to dissemination.

Once information reliability and consistency have been established, and reporting is more commonplace, this stage may not be required, particularly when the target audience and information are not sensitive or contentious.

4.6.2 Reporting environmental performance information

> The principal outputs from this section will be:
>
> o   The production of reports, presentations and communications
>
> o   The dissemination of reports, presentations and communications
>
> o   An analysis of feedback received.

Producing reports, presentations and communications

The production of reports, presentations and communications for all formats and audiences will require good planning and strong presentational skills in the media being used. In addition to this, the production lead-time of the reports needs to be consistent with meeting reporting schedules and deadlines.

At a simple level, information reported should be presented clearly, utilising visual aids to improve the impact and messages. The use of different font styles, charts, colour and illustrations can all be simply applied to enhance the most simple of information reports. However, do not make the report so busy that it detracts from the messages you want to convey.

Presentations will need strong presenting capability and high-impact media, as the communication of performance information in this way is often difficult to make interesting. This approach does, however, give the opportunity of allowing attendees to provide and receive feedback instantly which is more restricted when other approaches are used.

More-elaborate reports and communications such as:

- Brochure style reports
- Newsletters
- Posters
- On pack information
- Videos
- CD ROM

will usually require the greatest commitment in terms of resources, finance, time and planning. In addition to this, the skills and competencies required will be more specialised and might require outside assistance.

Given the high cost often associated with these communications, they should be considered carefully with respect to whether they are effective in reaching the target audience and in presenting the information and messages that you and the interested parties require. The format of these reporting approaches will also be less flexible in addressing the needs of diverse audiences and less open to changes in subsequent reports.

Use of intranet and internet facilities can offer a cheaper and more flexible approach, should elaborate reporting be required. This approach allows you to tailor reporting to the needs of a large number of interested parties through the use of different sections and pages, and password-protected areas. In addition the information is quicker and cheaper to update, and far more information can be provided. This forum also provides opportunity to establish an instant electronic feedback channel.

Specialist skills might be required here, both in the preparation and dissemination of the information, and in the accessing by the intended recipients. In assessing the use of more technical reporting methods, you should consider whether they will actually deliver to the intended audience. For example, reporting over the intranet is unlikely to reach operators with no proper access to intranet facilities or skills to use it.

A significant benefit of any EPE system is the ability to communicate relevant and reliable information on the environmental performance of the organisation to key interested parties. Reporting can add value to information generated by the EPE system if it is conducted well and in a timely manner, but can erode the value of information if poorly presented, late and/or irrelevant.

4.6.2.2 Disseminating reports, presentations and communications

The format of the reporting approach should have considered and identified the means by which the report is to be disseminated or delivered. It is important that this supports meeting reporting timescales in an achievable and cost-effective manner.

Where presentation approaches are being used, it will be important to ensure that arrangements are so made that presenters, facilities, equipment and materials are all available at a time and place which is suitable for the target audience. Note that this might be more time consuming and costly than the production of more elaborate remote report formats.

Remember to think of information as a product which if it is to maximise its potential worth needs to be in the:

* Right PLACE
* At the right TIME
* And in the right CONDITION.

4.6.2.3 Analysis of feedback received

We have already stressed the need for feedback channels to be provided (or in place) for the reporting process. Similarly it will be important to analyse any feedback received or actively solicited, in order to assess the views of interested parties with regard to:

- The environmental performance of the organisation
- The relevance and effectiveness of the EPE system
- The relevance and effectiveness of other environmental management tools and activity
- The value of the information reported and any future requirements
- The quality and effectiveness of the reporting format and approach adopted.

It is worth considering the motives of the parties who provide feedback, be this positive or negative. In addition, the level of feedback received might provide an insight into the effectiveness of the reporting format and approach and/or the feedback channel. In cases where feedback is limited or non-existent, this will probably require further investigation to determine whether the reporting or the feedback channel (or both) are in need of improvement, or if it is a cultural issue.

The outputs from feedback received will be fed into the review process established as part of the EPE system.

Section 4.6 checklist

Before you embark on the next stages of EPE implementation you should have:

○　　Determined the report format, content and schedule

○　　Gained approval to report information

○　　Produced reports, presentations and communications

○　　Disseminated reports, presentations and communications

○　　Analysed feedback received.

Chapter 5 Check and Act: Reviewing and Improving the EPE system

At the end of this chapter you should have covered and understood the main requirements for reviewing and improving the EPE system.

By following the tasks outlined, you will have established a regular review of the EPE system, in order to identify areas for development, maintenance and improvement.

The principal outputs of this chapter will be:

- The revision of the review structure, scope and schedule, and the development of review format(s)
- The establishment of an EPE review schedule, and detailed review specifications
- The implementation of the review process
- The monitoring and appraisal of the EPE system review process
- The creation of plans to implement remedial action, maintenance and improvements
- The dissemination of review process outputs to identified interested parties.

Task Heading	**Revising the review structure and schedule**
Section Reference	**5.1**
Duration	1 man day +
Difficulty Rating	1
Aims & Objectives	The aim of this section is to develop a structure of reviews and draw up a schedule. From this, a standard format (or formats) for the reviews of the EPE system can be developed.
	By following each stage of this section, you will produce the structure of reviews, a schedule, and have defined a format (or formats) to guide the review process.
Outputs	The principal outputs of this section will be:
	• A defined structure of EPE system review processes
	• A list of key parties required to participate in reviews
	• The identification of facility, equipment and location requirements
	• A schedule of EPE review processes
	• A format (or formats) for use as guidance in the different review processes.
Resources Considerations People	Project manager/EPE systems owner Project implementation team
Physical	Work station and office facilities Access to information on the availability of meeting attendees Information regarding other formal review or meeting structures, schedules and formats
Outputs from Previous Tasks	The implementation and operational plans. Sections 3.6.3 and 3.7.3 The reporting schedule. Section 4.6.1.1
Potential Problems	• Lack of management commitment to review process or agreed actions
	• Lack of resources and facilities
	• Lack of availability of key parties
	• Congested meeting or review timetables
	• Lack of project management skills or experience
	• Resistance to change and new ways of working
	• Resistance to formal structures and approaches.
Potential Opportunities	• Maintaining focus on key issues within the review process
	• Adopting, complementing or enhancing existing review processes
	• Interested parties having an input into the system design, operation and development.

5.1.1 Assessing the review structure and developing formats

> The principal outputs from this stage will be:
>
> ○ The revision of the structure and scope of reviews developed in the planning stage
>
> ○ The identification of parties who will be involved in the review process
>
> ○ The identification of facilities, equipment and location requirements of reviews
>
> ○ The revision of the review schedule
>
> ○ The development of review formats.

5.1.1.1 Revising the structure and scope of reviews

The structure and scope of the reviews that should be carried out to monitor the organisation's performance against environmental performance criteria, goals and targets, and the performance of the EPE system itself, were identified in section 3.6.1.4. Based upon experiences of the implementation phase it will be useful now to re-assess the review structure planned. This assessment should consider the number of reviews, the points (in the EPE system and the organisation) where reviews take place, and the scope of these reviews (i.e. what they cover), with a view to suitability.

Where reviews have been planned to support and interact with the reporting process, it will be necessary to consider the restrictions and requirements that this might impose on revision. For example, if a review is identified to vet information used for internal reporting of monthly results, then the review must take place in good time to allow compilation and distribution of the report information. Similarly, any revisions made should ensure that a coherent system of feeder and receiving reviews is maintained.

Appendix 19 provided a template on which to record the details of the structure and scope of reviews, and this will provide the basis for your revisions, along with any other structural flow charts or records developed. To support the process advised in this section Appendix 23 provides an additional template on which further detail of the revision can be recorded to create a review specification.

Identifying parties who will be involved in the review process

Where this has taken place at the planning stage, it will be necessary to review the parties to ensure that they are still required and/or whether additional parties might be needed. If the identification of parties has not taken place, then this will be required at this stage. Involved parties will generally come from within, or be contracted to, the organisation, but occasionally they may represent external interested parties. Where external interested parties are to be involved, there should be confidence in the relationship and the security of any information divulged.

The level of involvement of parties will vary according to the level of the review in the structure and whether they are required to:

- Participate
- Provide input
- Receive output, or
- Act upon output.

At this stage you might want to nominate individuals to be responsible for reviews (for each review or a number of reviews). However, this might be affected by the make-up of the review group, scheduling constraints and the format developed for the review process. For this reason the final decision on the review leaders is left until later on (see section 5.2.1.1).

In identifying parties Appendix 23 provides space to detail the individuals who will be participants, input providers and output receivers. It is likely that the individuals required to take action as a result of any review will be specified on a case by case basis, making prior identification unrealistic. In identifying participants, you should aim to include individuals who are involved with, or who can influence, the EPE system, in line with the scope of the review.

It is possible that specialist input might be required only for certain sections of the review or for particular reviews. In such cases the participants could be identified as part time or occasional. In other circumstances it may be difficult to ensure that a particular individual is always available, so you might specify a representative from a department or group.

You should attempt to build a balanced review group from individuals with the expertise, experience, skills and empowerment necessary, to be able to contribute effectively as a member of the review group. Review group members need to be in a position to commit to the review process, not only through attendance of review meetings, but also in undertaking actions coming from the review. Senior managers may find it difficult truly to give this level of commitment, so although they may seem the best person for the review group, alternatives might need to be considered.

Review groups should also be manageable in terms of numbers. What numbers are manageable will depend upon the format of the review, availability and the skill of the review leader in co-ordinating the activity of the review group. You will need to try to strike a balance between spread of inputs and the manageability of the group.

Finally, the template provides space to nominate a minute taker. While this may not be appropriate for all review formats, it is suggested that identifying a minute taker will assist with the documentation of reviews and agreed actions. It can be advantageous to have the minutes recorded by someone who is not directly involved in the review, albeit that some knowledge of the area will be useful.

5.1.1.3 Identifying facilities, equipment and location required for reviews

Once the structure of reviews and the participants have been identified it will be necessary to identify the requirements for facilities, equipment and location for each review, as this can impact upon the review scheduling and will be needed when implementing the review process. Where specialist facilities, equipment or locations are required, it is likely that these will need arranging well in advance. If this is the case, special note should be made of this on the review specification (see Appendix 23).

5.1.1.4 Revising the review schedule

The original schedule of reviews produced in sections 3.6.1.4 and 3.7.2.6 is likely to require revision, especially if the structure and scope of reviews were revised in section 5.1.1.1. The schedule developed can be amended as necessary, and Appendix 23 provides space to identify the timings of each review.

If revising the review schedule, care should be taken to ensure that the timings of feeder reviews, the review in question and any receiving reviews are compatible. In addition, any reporting processes linked into the review should be considered. If special facilities, equipment or locations are required, then this could also impose restrictions on the schedule that require consideration.

Schedules should allow time for:

- Inputs prior to the review
- Dissemination of outputs
- Action to be taken on the outputs
- Feedback to be received prior to the next review.

If the intervals between reviews are too short, then the review can become meaningless and time consuming. However, if the interval is too great, it is easy to lose continuity, momentum and control over performance and agreed actions, so that, for example, the actions agreed at a previous review may be irrelevant by the time the next review is held. Again, you must seek the best balance for the organisation and the circumstances, but remember that schedules and timings can always be altered as the EPE system matures and experience is gained.

Finally, the participants identified in section 5.1.1.2 will all have varying degrees of availability, and this can present restrictions on the scheduling of reviews. This might relate to levels of activity within the organisation (e.g. seasonal peaks, annual stock-taking, end of financial year, shift handover), so time of year, month or day may be an important consideration when scheduling. In the event that no suitable time can be allotted for all proposed participants, then alternative solutions or compromises should be sought. Do not scrap a planned review because it is too difficult or inconvenient, unless there is no alternative.

5.1.1.5 Developing the review formats

This stage looks at the development of a format for each review that will help:

- Define the manner in which the review is conducted
- Ensure that the prescribed scope of the review is covered
- Provide a robust mechanism for the allocation of agreed actions
- Track implementation and closure of agreed actions.

The manner in which the review is conducted will to some extent be shaped by the review leader, but depending upon the skills and experience of this individual some degree of guidance may prove useful. The key features of the format should cover:

- The nature of the review, e.g. meeting, discussion group, questionnaire, electronic exchange, one to one consultations
- The length of the review
- The subject areas to be covered as routine, by order

- Detail of any occasional subject areas to be covered, and when
- Any information required for review or to assist review
- The method and style of recording the proceedings
- The style and timing of the output provided to participants and nominated recipients
- The style and timing of the output fed through to other reviews or reporting processes
- The nature of any feedback mechanisms to support the review
- Detail of any events to take place as routine or occasionally (e.g. guest presentation or specific subject assessments).

The review can be kept within the defined scope by identifying subject areas to be covered, while the allocation, tracking, implementation and closure of agreed actions can be controlled by clearly identifying, in the recording of proceedings, individual responsibility and timescales.

Defining the style and timing of review outputs can help to minimise disruption to dependent reviews and reports, and to individuals tasked with actions from the reviews.

Section 5.1 checklist

Before you embark on the next stages of EPE implementation you should have:

O   Revised the structure and scope of reviews developed in the planning stage

O   Identified parties, facilities, equipment and locations that will be involved in the review process

O   Revised the review schedule

O   Developed review formats.

Task Heading	**Implementing the EPE review schedule**
Section Reference	**5.2**
Duration	4 man days +
Difficulty Rating	3
Aims & Objectives	The aim of this section is to implement the schedule for reviewing the EPE system.
	By following each stage of this section you will have implemented a structure and schedule of system reviews involving key participating parties (see section 5.1.1). The reviews will follow the formats developed under section 5.1.1.5 in order to review thoroughly the EPE system, identify areas for improvement and receive feedback.
Outputs	The principal outputs of this section will be:
	• The identification of a representative to be responsible for the review process
	• The notification of the structure, schedule and formats of reviews to all parties
	• Inviting input from identified interested parties
	• Gathering information for the review
	• Conducting the review process
	• The monitoring of review timings, attendance and outputs
	• The appraisal of the suitability of review structures, schedules and formats
	• The recording and retention of review proceedings and outputs
	• Identifying actions and planning requirements
	• Dissemination of review process outputs to identified interested parties.
Resources Considerations People	Project manager/EPE system owner Project implementation team Top management Functional and operational management Other key interested parties, e.g. suppliers, customers, insurers, investors Administrational support
Physical	Work station and office facilities Meeting facilities Availability of information and reports generated Communications networks Access to presentation materials, equipment and media
Outputs from Previous Tasks	The implementation and operational plans. Sections 3.6.3 and 3.7.3 Structure and schedule of the EPE system review processes. Section 5.1.1 List of key parties required to participate in reviews, provide input and receive feedback. Section 5.1.1.2 Formats for use as guidance in the different review processes. Section 5.1.1.5
Potential Problems	• Lack of commitment to review process
	• Lack of review process management skills available to the organisation
	• Hidden agendas
	• Inadequate time allocated to reviewing. the EPE system and outputs

	• Excessive amount of effort spent on reviewing as opposed to taking action • Over-bureaucratic and over-lengthy review processes.
Potential Opportunities	• Regular check on progress, providing chance to identify and rectify problems • Building awareness and understanding • Maintaining focus on performance as a regular activity • Potential to enhance the system • Interested parties having an input into the system • Providing a network by which to disseminate EPE information.

5.2.1 Preparing for implementation

> The principal outputs from this stage will be:
>
> O The identification of review leaders
>
> O The notification of the review schedule and formats to parties involved
>
> O The arrangement of facilities and communications media
>
> O The invitation of input from interested parties
>
> O Gathering information for the review.

5.2.1.1 Identifying review leaders

It will be important to nominate a review leader for each review forum scheduled. The review leader will be responsible for ensuring:

- That reviews are conducted in line with the schedule
- That nominated participants are active within the review process
- That any required facilities and equipment are provided
- That reviews cover all necessary areas as defined by the scope and format
- That required actions identified are agreed, planned, implemented and completed
- That relevant information and input are gathered prior to reviews
- That review proceedings are accurately recorded
- That relevant information and agreed actions are communicated to interested parties, as identified, within scheduled timescales
- That any information required for reporting is communicated to the relevant parties within scheduled timescales
- That feedback provision is in place, and that feedback is evaluated as part of the review process
- That feedback is given to the EPE team on the review process, the outputs, successes and difficulties.

Normally, the review leader will remain the same in order to give some consistency to the process and proceedings. Review leaders should have been identified as a participant of the review forum, but where the skills and competencies to conduct the leadership are not present it might be necessary to introduce a participant specifically for this purpose (e.g. the environmental manager, an operations manager, a team leader). However, eventual handover of leadership responsibility to a regular participant is advised for such circumstances.

As with participants, review leaders will need to be able to commit time and effort to the process, and in many cases this will be over and above the requirements of a regular participant. This must be considered when selecting a review leader, and could require that a less senior leader is nominated (i.e. less senior in the organisation's hierarchy). This highlights the need for the review leader to have the authority to make decisions relating to the review forum and the outputs of the review.

The review leader should possess a good understanding of the scope that the review encompasses, as well as good communication, presentation and organisational skills. Experience with the EPE system and managing review processes will also be useful. Prescriptive review formats can avoid the need for such strong skills among review leaders and may well prove the most realistic option, especially in the early stages of the process. Additionally, training and guidance should be provided to help review leaders.

5.2.1.2 Notifying involved parties

In implementing the review process, it will be necessary to notify all involved parties of the review structure, schedule (including time and location), scope of reviews, and what will be required of them. This notification will need to be given in good time in order to allow for feedback and/or preparation.

It may well be necessary to arrange facilities and equipment (as identified in the review specification) in advance of this notification, if these require advance notice.

5.2.1.3 Inviting input from interested parties

As part of the notification process, it will also be important, a suitable time ahead of the review, to invite input from any parties identified for providing input. Where input is vital for the scope of the review, this might need to be solicited actively, and for this resources and time may need to be made available.

In most cases the interested parties who will provide input to the review process will be internal to the organisation. Where information is sought from external interested parties, greater effort and/or diplomacy might be required. Examples of external interested parties who might provide information are listed below.

* Partners in environmental initiatives
* Suppliers
* Customers
* Industry bodies and trade associations
* Enforcement bodies
* Investors
* Insurers
* Research bodies.

Developing an indicator to show how well information providers perform might prove a useful planning and motivational tool at this stage.

5.2.1.4 Gathering information for the review

In similar vein to the invitation of input from interested parties, it will also be necessary for the review leader (or appointed participant) to gather information which will be relevant for the review. The nature of this information, and the quality of documentation systems, will determine how much time and effort will be required for this task.

The review format should specify any information required in the review on a routine basis, and as the process develops so other information requirements will become apparent.

Some key pieces of information that will be required (as relevant to the scope of the review) are listed below.

* Records of the previous review(s)
* The latest environmental performance information and previous information as deemed necessary
* Environmental performance criteria, goals, objectives and targets
* Outputs from the analysis and assessment of environmental performance data
* Records of verification activity conducted
* Any relevant reports
* Records of any alterations or amendments made to the EPE system since the last review
* Feedback on relevant aspects of the EPE system.

5.2.2   Conducting implementation

> The principal outputs from this stage will be:
>
> O   Conducting the reviews
>
> O   The monitoring and appraisal of the reviews
>
> O   The recording of review proceedings
>
> O   The identification of actions and planning requirements
>
> O   The dissemination of outputs from the review process.

5.2.2.1   Conducting reviews

Reviews should be conducted in line with the schedule developed in section 5.1.1.4, and it should be the responsibility of the review leader to ensure that this happens. Note that if a number of levels of review exist in the structure and/or reporting is dependent on review outputs, then any delays will have a knock-on effect through the schedule.

Section 5.2.1.1 identified the responsibilities of the review leader, which will need upholding when conducting reviews.

The following list identifies possible questions which might assist the review leader in conducting the reviews.

* Is the EPE system providing adequate information to assess the organisation's environmental performance?
* Is the EPE system providing adequate information to report on the organisation's environmental performance to the interested parties identified?
* Is the EPE system providing relevant and useful information to management?
* Is the EPE system being operated in accordance with developed schedules, procedures and practices?
* How well has the EPE system integrated with other systems in the organisation?
* Are there any requirements for further procedures or schedules, training and support?
* How valuable is the feedback being received?
* Are the timescales established and resources committed adequate?
* What is the progress towards the targets, objectives, goals and criteria set?
* Is the EPE system adding value to the organisation?
* How can the EPE system be improved?

- What changes or new challenges will the EPE system have to accommodate now and in the future?

5.2.2.2 Monitoring and appraising reviews

Part of the review leader's responsibilities noted in section 5.2.1.1 is the feedback of information on the review process, the outputs, successes and difficulties. It will be important for the EPE team to monitor and appraise the various reviews to establish where they are successful, but probably more importantly where they are not producing satisfactory results. Some indicators can be established to gauge the performance of the reviews on a number of criteria such as:

- The timeliness of reviews against the schedule
- The percentage attendance of nominated participants
- The performance record for clearing off action points within agreed timescales
- The timeliness of communicating review minutes.

Reviews that are not performing well will need appraising to establish required action. This might take the form of support or empowerment for the review leader, changes to the review format, development of skills for the leader or within the group, or possibly a change of participants.

5.2.2.3 Recording review proceedings

Throughout this section we have referred to the recording of review proceedings. This is an important part of the EPE system, as it will provide a record of key performance issues, the health of the EPE system, agreed actions, and progress made within the system and in environmental performance management overall.

When reviews take the form of formal meetings, it is customary to produce minutes. However, alternative review formats (e.g. oral briefings, electronic discussion groups) will need recording by some means as well.

Recording the review proceedings is often viewed as being laborious, time consuming and bureaucratic, but without accurate records of proceedings you are likely to lose control of the EPE system, and fail to counter threats or realise opportunities effectively. Records, of some form, will be required if demonstrable continual improvement is required.

5.2.2.4 Identifying actions and planning requirements

The key to driving continual improvement in environmental performance and in the EPE system itself will be the identification of additional action from the review process. Action can be:

- Remedial – to correct defects
- Investigative – undertaking research of the issue or area
- Exploratory – conducting tests and trials
- Enhancing – seeking to improve on the existing situation.

It is important that reviews agree actions as key outputs, which can then be fed back into the PDCA cycle. Individuals, or possibly groups, should be allocated responsibility for seeing through agreed actions, and timescales should be also be defined. In some instances it might be necessary to impose other restrictions, such as resource use or the level of impact on other areas of the system or organisation.

Some actions agreed will be straightforward (e.g. changing a data collection form, replacing a simple piece of measurement equipment) and others will be involved (extensive retraining, implementing a new communications system), requiring careful planning and possibly approval and commitment from senior management.

Feeding agreed actions back through the PDCA cycle should ensure that all necessary considerations and steps are made.

5.2.2.5 Disseminating outputs from the review process

The final step of the review process will be to disseminate outputs. In this context outputs can be defined as:

- Agreed actions, and associated plans, timescales and conditions
- Approved revisions to schedules, plans, instructions, guidance, procedures or practices
- Information for reporting processes
- Records of proceedings (to prescribed parties)
- Review leader feedback
- Any other noteworthy information.

The dissemination of outputs should be efficient enough to provide interested parties with clear and reliable information in line with scheduled timescales.

Section 5.2 checklist

Before you embark on the next stages of EPE implementation you should have:

O   Identified review leaders

O   Notified the review schedule and formats to parties involved

O   Arranged facilities and communications media

O   Invited input from interested parties and gathered information for the review

O   Conducted the reviews in line with the schedule

O   Monitored and appraised the reviews

O   Recorded the review proceedings

O   Identified actions and planning requirements

O   Disseminated the outputs from the review process.

Chapter 6 *Applications of ISO14031*

This guidebook has looked at the requirements for establishing an ISO14031 EPE system, in order to help you track and manage the environmental issues, aspects and impacts of your organisation, alongside, or independently of, any other environmental management activity.

Throughout the guidebook there have been references made to further applications of ISO14031 and EPE systems, to assist you in managing various areas of environmental management. The scope of these subjects is too large, however, to embark on any in-depth explanation and guidance for these applications within this guidebook, but this chapter will outline some of the principal characteristics and considerations of an ISO14031 EPE system for the following applications:

* Using ISO14031 with ISO14001
* ISO14031 as a stand-alone tool
* Benchmarking
* Project evaluation
* Environmental-risk assessment
* Environmental communications and reporting
* Cleaner production
* Highlighting product attributes
* Environmental supply-chain management
* Environmental accounting.

6.1 Using ISO14031 with ISO14001

As already identified in this book, there are clear benefits for environmental management systems to be derived from the application of EPE systems. ISO14031 has been designed as a value-adding supplement to the ISO14001 EMS model. Indeed, ISO14031 was developed with the ISO14001 standard in mind, and the EPE model takes on many of the characteristics of the core EMS elements described within ISO14001 (see Figure 42). While ISO14031 will undoubtedly bring benefits to any formal EMS, the close ties with ISO14001 inevitably make this the most compatible pairing. The latest revision of EMAS will bring this scheme closer to ISO14031 as well, given that the revision was aimed at bringing EMAS more in line with ISO14001.

Figure 42   **Relationship between ISO14031 and ISO14001**

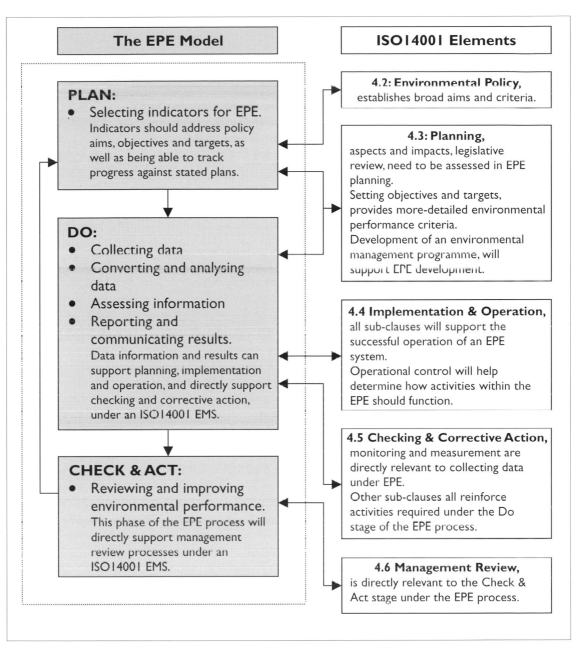

(Adapted from Figure 1, ISO14031, 1999, p.4)

The application of ISO14031 alongside ISO14001 will help your organisation in achieving or maintaining EMS certification by focusing efforts on the defined aims (stated in your policy), objectives and targets of your organisation, through the use of quantifiable and reportable performance measures. The EPE system, by providing tangible information about the organisation's environmental performance, will assist the environmental management function in tracking performance and identifying further action. This in turn will help the organisation demonstrate continual improvement, to which it must have committed itself as a requirement of the ISO14001 standard.

Further to this, in an ISO14031 demonstration project in the UK, the ISO14031 EPE approach was found to help organisations identify and understand the cause and effect relationships for activities, products and services more clearly than through work with ISO14001 alone. This will also help build understanding of the significance of environmental aspects and/or impacts.

If you already have a mature EMS system, ISO14031 can help to shift emphasis from system maintenance to actual performance improvements. You will already understand your key issues and will probably find the development of suitable indicators which reflect performance a relatively straightforward process. Alternatively, if you are embarking on the implementation of an ISO14001 certifiable EMS, then the application of ISO14031 at the early stages will provide a clear focus and means of monitoring progress, in terms of both environmental performance and the environmental management system. The full value of an ISO14031 EPE system will generally only be realised some time after its implementation (i.e. once sufficient data and information have been produced), so the earlier you start, the sooner you will reap the rewards.

Case Example   An extract of findings from a UK government sponsored ISO14031 demonstration project (2000), conducted by 14000 & ONE Solutions Ltd

For the companies involved in the project who were seeking to develop EMSs with a view to attaining certification to ISO14001, all were at the very early stages of EMS development, having produced an environmental policy, primarily in response to customer demands.

In view of this, the ISO14031 approach knitted well with the aspirations of the companies involved, in that it focuses on areas required by ISO14001. The concept of performance indicators had been established in all of the companies, and therefore the concept of developing an EPE system for environmental management was readily accepted.

Organisations implementing an ISO14001 EMS identified where the ISO14031 EPE approach provided benefits, by:

* Providing a clear focus for the organisation's environmental management efforts, helping to quantify objectives and targets, and driving continual improvement of performance

---

- Providing an indication of environmental risk faced by the organisation

- Giving an indication of the significance of aspects and impacts

- Helping to track costs and revenues associated with environmental activities

- Providing information for the comparison of divisional performance

- Providing motivation for different parties within the organisation

- Focusing attention on root causes and subsequent impacts

- Helping to identify where controls and procedures are required

- Providing substantial information for internal communication, reporting, and the management review process.

The EPE programmes developed were all held to be practical and value adding. Although the majority of indicators developed would require procedural or systems development, much of this work would be required under ISO14001 anyway, and where it was not, the value of the indicator outputs was deemed to justify the effort.

6.1.1 Tracking the EMS development process

Management performance indicators (MPIs) can be developed to track the progress of EMS development and implementation. To develop this tool it is important to understand the steps or path followed towards the development and implementation of the EMS. This set of indicators could be based on the necessary steps as planned for the implementation of the EMS.

In applying indicators in this manner, you should develop clear instructions for the assessment of progress so as to ensure output of consistent and reliable information. Once the EMS is operational, the EPE principles can still be used to track ongoing performance.

The application of indicators in this scenario can be developed to track the progress of sections, departments, functions, business units, divisions or locations, as well as for the organisation as a whole. This will provide some indication of resource or commitment issues during implementation, and can be used as the basis for reported information and motivating different parties. Scoring, weighting and aggregation of indicator information could also prove useful for assessment and reporting purposes.

6.1.2   EPE influences over EMS

If EMS and EPE development and operation run in conjunction, the EPE can have a number of influences over the EMS approach. In addition to providing information to track performance and progress, the EPE system can help identify where controls are needed, the level of environmental-risk exposure, legal compliance record, training needs, and aspects and impacts significance, and facilitate reporting and greater awareness and understanding. Further influences that can add value and strengthen the EMS are described below.

6.1.2.1   EMS and performance

The process of EPE strengthens the focus of the EMS on performance, so that it is not solely about a management system that meets the initial set of requirements needed to gain certification. This is important, as, increasingly, interested parties are having doubts as to whether ISO14001 certification provides enough assurance of strong environmental performance.

> **Case Example   BAE Systems: using EPE to track and report EMS contributions to financial performance**
>
> *BAE Systems is a multinational defence equipment and systems developer and manufacturer operating sites in the UK and with partnership ventures worldwide.*
>
> *BAE Systems' site at Samlesbury (which encompasses three separate business units) gained certification to ISO14001 in 1997. In order to demonstrate the contribution of the EMS, and track performance, the environmental management team started to develop an EPE system based on the draft ISO14031 standard guidance.*
>
> *An indicator relating to costs and benefits resulting from environmental projects was established to demonstrate the net financial contribution. This contribution in 1997/98 amounted to £485,000 from 35 separate projects. By providing tangible output data the EPE has strengthened the internal reporting process and it is an aim of the company to report in greater detail externally.*
>
> *After operating the ISO14031 EPE system alongside the ISO14001 EMS for nearly two years at the Samlesbury site, the team have found that the process has focused attention throughout the business on key environmental issues. As a result of this, the organisation has managed to identify significant cost-saving projects across the site and has managed to improve environmental performance, against established criteria, consistently over time.*

6.1.2.2   Raising awareness and increasing interest

EPE can have influence during the EMS development by raising awareness in different ways. The immediate need for data drives the involvement of people more quickly and in a more direct and evident way than with EMS. With EMS, involvement could stay at a conceptual level for quite a while, reducing people's interest. This gives an edge to EPE as a more practical approach that could be more attractive to some people compared to EMS alone – although in some instances the culture of the organisation may be resistant to measurement and quantification. Furthermore, the process of developing indicators can increase the value of currently available data, improving understanding and providing an additional dimension to the contribution of those generating and gathering the data.

6.1.2.3   Significance evaluation

Information provided by EPE could influence the identification of significant aspects and impacts (as required under ISO14001) by providing real, tangible data, as opposed to relying on estimated or assumed information.

> ## Case Example   ICI: the environmental burden approach to assessing the significance of environmental impacts
>
> *ICI is a large multinational chemical company producing a wide variety of products, all contributing to a complex range of environmental aspects and impacts.*
>
> ICI soon realised that the measurement, monitoring and reporting of perform-ance indicators in absolute terms, such as tonnes or numbers of chemicals emitted was limited, insofar as it provided little understanding of the true envi-ronmental impact of emissions. In recognition of this ICI began working to develop the Environmental burden (EB) approach, which is 'a way to rank the potential environmental impact of ... different emissions' against seven 'global environmental impact categories' (ICI, 1997).
>
> * Acidity
> * Global warming
> * Human health effects (airborne carcinogens)
> * Ozone depletion
> * Photochemical ozone creation
> * Aquatic oxygen demand
> * Ecotoxicity to aquatic life
>
> Within the environmental-impact categories, the potential impact that each sub-stance has in each category was ranked. This ranking is referred to as the potency factor (PF) and is expressed as a factor of a common base unit. As an example, for global warming CO_2 is used as the base unit with an index global warming potential (GWP) of one, and all other substances which can con-tribute to global warming are then given a GWP factor related to CO_2 . Thus, methane, which is potentially twenty-one times as potent as CO_2 in global warming, has a PF of twenty-one. The potency factor is then multiplied by the actual amount of each substance released for each category upon which that substance has a potential impact.
>
> The EB approach, by enabling comparison of potential impacts, provides a use-ful insight into the significance of actions and products, and thus will facilitate the identification of a clear focus for environmental management activity.
>
> (Sources: ISO14031, 1999 and *Environmental Burden: The ICI Approach,* 1997.)

6.1.2.4   Relationships to quality management systems (QMSs)

Many ISO9000 quality management systems are perceived to be bureau-cratic, and only the maturity of the QMS, brought about by its continuing use and an emphasis on performance improvement over time, has resulted in streamlining of the system.

It is a concern of management that ISO14001 should not follow the same initial path as ISO9000, and especially that people should not perceive ISO14001 as just another bureaucratic exercise.

Information generated by an EPE system could provide an objective view of EMS performance. In the past, improvements in the QMS came about more through qualitative assessment and attention to areas of weakness highlighted by auditing (internal and external). EPE can provide tangible information as well to support the identification of improvement activity, and will increase the chances of recognising problems before they become serious incidents. In this vein, the use of the EPE model might also be used to identify quality-performance indicators. Such approaches may even lead to new ideas in management system integration where core elements of quality, environment and health and safety management are fully integrated, with sets of performance data then being reviewed and managed accordingly.

6.1.2.5 Operational EMS as support to EPE operation

Once the EMS is operational, it can provide a more robust managerial infrastructure to support the operation, review and development of the EPE system. The EPE system developments will in turn support the EMS in becoming more effective, thus creating a strong interdependence between the two approaches. It will be advantageous to consider both ISO14001 and ISO14031 as contributing to one environmental management system, as opposed to two separate systems.

6.2 ISO14031 as a stand-alone environmental management tool

With the development of the ISO14031 guidance standard being closely linked to the ISO14001 EMS standard, the benefits of applying the two standards in conjunction are clear. However, there are also benefits to be realised by organisations who do not have or wish to develop a formal EMS. In this context ISO14031 can be applied independently of any formal EMS, albeit that some elements of the approach will be consistent with or similar to elements required under ISO14001.

The value of applying ISO14031 as a stand-alone environmental management approach revolves around focusing on environmental performance issues within a flexible framework which is potentially less prescriptive and bureaucratic than systems developed under ISO14001. This flexibility allows you to develop the system as much or as little as you believe to be necessary (or as time and resources will permit). But remember, ISO14031 is not a certifiable standard, and thus cannot provide the same level of externally verified assurance that ISO14001 can. Your interested parties will determine how important this is, but indeed you might find that they are more interested in real environmental performance than the ability to operate a conforming management system. In view of this, the reporting element of ISO14031 will become very much more important for stand-alone EPE systems.

Recognising the flexibility which exists for stand-alone ISO14031 EPE systems, this section will look at two scenarios at the extremes, namely, a simple approach, and a detailed approach.

6.2.1 The simple approach

In the simple approach, an organisation brainstorms environmental pressures, aspects and impacts to identify all environmental issues. Through this process, the significant environmental aspects and issues are identified. For significant aspects and issues, one or two indicators (usually OPIs and MPIs) are developed, and the environmental performance criteria also agreed. Improvement initiatives are then established with timeframes and the indicators are used to determine the progress of these initiatives.

The PDCA model is used to drive improvements in environmental performance related to the significant aspects on a continual basis. It is likely that information will need to be built up over a period of time before targets can be quantified.

In this approach, one or two persons co-ordinate the ISO14031-based EPE, with support for the improvement initiatives being extended from the rest of the organisation. There are very few systems elements such as procedures and documentation. The focus is on using indicators to bring about direct improvements in environmental performance. The importance of reporting the performance information will be raised under the simple approach, because you will not have a lot of documented evidence to support any claims to undertaking environmental activity.

6.2.2 The detailed approach

Using a more detailed approach, an organisation identifies aspects and impacts in a manner similar to an ISO14001-based EMS. The assessment of key environmental issues and pressures, as well as features of the organisation, will be comprehensive and detailed. Clear goals and direction for the programme will be developed and significant aspects and impacts will be identified through the use of a systematic approach (but not necessarily in line with ISO14001 certification requirements).

Selection of indicators will be developed to support the goals and direction established, and targets will probably be established as the basis for indicators, or as a result of indicators developed. MPIs will be used heavily to provide control over the system processes and plans, and this will in turn support the review process established to maintain and improve the EPE system.

Often the more detailed the approach the greater the need for it to be supported by elements of the traditional management systems model, such as training records, documentation, procedures, objectives, etc. With this in mind it is easy to see how ISO14031 might be used as a stepping-stone to a fully certified EMS.

The more detailed the ISO14031 EPE system adopted, the more likely it is to bring greater benefits in the long run. However, this will depend on the system focusing on the key issues, and will probably involve more resources and commitment.

6.3 Benchmarking

Recently, there has been a trend towards benchmarking performance within both the private and public sectors. Whether on environmental issues or other key operational functions, organisations are increasingly interested in setting, or required to set, their performance against others' on certain issues.

ISO14031 can be used as a tool for internal or external benchmarking, so as to compare environmental performance between different entities, be they sites, departments, cost-centres, companies or economic sectors. By the comparison of environmental performance between such entities it is hoped to encourage the sharing of information and best practice, to motivate managers and staff to achieve better performance, and to inform management of areas in which to focus activity.

This section will look at external and internal benchmarking separately.

6.3.1 External benchmarking

In terms of environmental management practices, an increase in general awareness levels and a more sophisticated understanding of the major environmental issues facing society have led to an upturn in the requirements for organisations to report their environmental performance to third parties. Inevitably, this has resulted in comparisons between their operational characteristics. Ultimately, organisations are finding their performance being compared against that of their peers, industry best practice and other benchmarks.

Whether an organisation is benchmarking its own performance, or that of other institutions, comparisons are greatly assisted through the availability of reliable, tangible information. Organisations are under increasing pressure to produce, collate or compare environmental performance information. However, this has proved to be extremely challenging to date. As an example, how would you compare two organisations from different sectors? Even if they are from the same sector, how do you make allowances for their differing size, location or production characteristics?

These are questions that many organisations are attempting to answer. There are a number of environmental benchmarking initiatives underway at the moment. In the UK the Business in the Environment group has developed an Index of Corporate Environmental Engagement (BiE 2000). This index uses a number of environmental management performance criteria to compare the level of environmental engagement among the top 350 quoted UK companies, as this tends to apply more generically than operational performance. The index ranks the companies based on a weighted scoring system and the results are published on an annual basis. The index has concentrated on environmental management performance criteria due to the difficulties encountered when trying to compare performance for operational criteria between sectors, but attempts are being made to increasingly focus on operational performance criteria.

A number of organisations have developed guidelines for producing corporate environmental reports (e.g. Global Reporting Initiative, DETR Guidance, Responsible Care, UNEP) and these tend to cover what type of indicators are to be included. Although most only offer a loose guidance, it might be worth investigating if the companies that you might wish to benchmark yourself against are using any of these guidelines in their reports. You might also need to consider what indicators they are using, if they have made any specific definitions of their indicators or made detailed explanation of how are they measured.

However, what is clear is that not all environmental criteria are relevant to all sectors. As a result, data comparison is often only meaningful between organisations from the same sector or with the same characteristics. Data also need to be normalised, with variable factors taken into account and relevant weighting or bias applied. Such data may be available from sector bodies or industrial associations and can be extremely useful as a guide to the types of environmental performance criteria one might consider in the development of an EPE system.

ISO14031 can be used in sector-specific industry associations as a means to undertake the benchmarking of their member companies on their environmental performance, since it offers an excellent framework for developing indicators for such performance. Sector-specific industry associations provide a variety of services to their member companies and environmental performance benchmarking is emerging as one such service. This can contribute to improving the competitiveness of the member companies and therefore the industry as a whole. The benchmarking service will involve establishing a database of the sector-specific indicators. This database will contain data against environmental parameters that are identified as relevant for the particular industry sector.

Based on this data indices can be established within ISO14031 indicator methodology. Those parties interested in understanding where an organisation stands in comparison to industry average or best practice can submit their data to the industry association and obtain a comparison. Alternatively, benchmark data might be provided (possibly at some charge) and this can be built in to the performance criteria and targets under the EPE system.

Information required by government could also be translated into environmental performance indicators and used for benchmarking. This would lead to a consistency of approach and give some degree of reliability to the data. However, this would then only be practical when comparing organisations operating under the same governmental guidance.

If externally developed indicators are to be adopted, it is important to know their specification, that is the data used, how and when they are collected, what conversion is applied and the tolerances allowed. Although the indicators might have similar titles, they might include different information. Furthermore, measuring methods are also important, as two disparate measuring methods could result in significantly different information, having different precision and/or accuracy.

One thing that is important in all of this is the reliability of the data and the methods used in their collation. By using an accepted and standardised approach to EPE and reporting, it follows that the margin of error and the reliability of the data should improve.

6.3.2 Internal benchmarking

Benchmarking environmental performance across internal entities can be an effective tool for establishing relative performance and commitment, as well as providing a means of motivating those responsible to improve. In the same way as external benchmarking processes need to be consistent and equitable, so internal schemes should strive for this. However, internal management culture may be more tolerant of some inequity in the process if the outcome of such schemes is to motivate performance improvement.

Consistency of approach will be easier to achieve internally, as the methodology and approach used are directly under the control of the organisation's management. Similarly, collating information on performance can be achieved more quickly and at less cost, thus enabling more-frequent comparison of performance. Automated data collection and communication systems may even allow for real-time performance comparison, if this is deemed of use.

Where benchmarking between entities in an organisation is not seen as appropriate, due to large differences in the activities, products, services or operational circumstances, it might be more appropriate to benchmark performance over time. In this case you would need to develop a reliable basis of historical data first, and the entity should not be subject a great degree of frequent change, if any sensible conclusions are to drawn.

As with external benchmarking the indicators most suited to cross comparison tend to be MPIs, as management efforts tend to be more generic than operational conditions.

6.4 Project evaluation

There is an increasing requirement to predict and track the net environmental impact associated with projects or policy change. For example, waste minimisation projects, capital investment in abatement technology, or a policy decision to recover products at end of life from customers.

The EPE system can provide data and information that might assist in the preparation of more thorough and accurate forecasts, as well as providing a means for tracking performance of the project or policy decision. By developing headline indicators which track performance in the main areas for potential impact, the manager of the programme can quickly assess the effectiveness of the project against predictions, and identify problems that may be caused by the activity in question.

The reporting of the project performance can be in terms of OPIs, MPIs and ECIs that can be mutually agreed as part of the project delivery parameters. Such information might then be collated with that from other projects so that the project sponsor might centrally report on the environmental performance improvements (or otherwise) associated with their work. Linking forecast and actual performance indicators to financial costs and benefits will further assist in justifying environmental initiatives, or deciding between alternatives.

6.5 Environmental risk assessment

The EPE system can provide for the development of indicators that will help in the assessment of the level of environmental risk faced by an organisation. In practice these indicators will tend to fall into four categories:

- Reflective
- Predictive
- Hazard
- Commercial.

Reflective risk indicators are commonly applied, especially by third parties, when assessing an organisation's level of exposure. These indicators tend to focus on past performance, such as the number of incidents or the number of prosecutions. While continually poor results will suggest poor management, a good track record does not mean that this organisation is any less at risk. Indeed, complacency might even make this organisation a higher risk proposition.

The only way that risk can be truly assessed is to focus on the factors which increase the probability of an adverse occurrence, or the actual hazard itself. Probability can be assessed through the use of predictive indicators, which attempt to measure factors that can influence the likelihood of an occurrence. For example, recording the number of emergency preparedness and response drills conducted per period gives some indication of the risk of incidents being dealt with adequately. Monitoring the number of customer environmental criteria applied to contracts might indicate the risk of losing business in the event of an environmental incident.

Indicators of environmental exposure tend to be MPIs, and commonly focus on compliance with legal and contractual requirements, with prevention measures, response effectiveness, training and reporting receiving most attention. However, financial risk exposure through potential taxation, and market price and exchange rate volatility, can also be assessed through the use of tracking indicators.

Hazard indicators will seek to measure the extent of a recognised hazard, and any change to this over time. For example, the reduced consumption of a hazardous material would indicate a lower overall risk. Alternatively, changes to the material specification might reduce the hazard and consequently the risk (all other things remaining constant).

Risk assessments can be assimilated to cost information, such as fines, clean-up costs, increased insurance premiums and lost materials, or the impact on the worth of the organisation through damage to reputation. Indicators developed to help assess exposure to environmental risk are likely to prove valuable tools to the organisation's management.

The use of current incident-related costs as an indicator of risk is reflective, but here you can aim to use the level of these costs to justify resource allocation to managing down the risks. Demonstrated savings can not only be offset against risk management costs but also prove the effectiveness of the risk management regime internally and externally. A case exists for indexing these costs to a base year, however, given that successful risk management, over time, will erode the very argument upon which it is built.

6.6   Environmental communications and reporting

The fact that an ISO14031 EPE system produces tangible information that is relevant to the key environmental issues, aspects and impacts of your organisation will inevitably help you in communicating meaningful and accurate information to your interested parties, both internally and externally.

Corporate environmental reports (CERs) can be supported using ISO14031 indicators. Such reports often include management performance, operational performance and environmental condition information. EPE information can focus on the views of interested parties (which is the very audience you should be reporting to). Very often CERs contain lots of environmental data that are not relevant to the audience which reads them, or which do not address the concerns of interested parties. ISO14031 provides a great opportunity to increase the value of such reports, improving relationships and image, through good consultation that leads to well-focused reports.

ISO14031 also requires that you develop indicators that are based on your significant aspects and/or impacts. Thus, using this framework to produce environmental performance data will ensure that you have at least considered your significant aspects and/or impacts and are tracking performance with a view to improvement. Currently, there is general criticism that many CERs have no relevance to the main issues of the reporting organisation. Insubstantial reporting of this nature can prove counter-productive. The specialist environmental press now regularly review and critique public CERs. This level of scrutiny means that you can no longer risk a slip-up in your data management and reporting processes. Using ISO14031 should help you to ensure that information is consistent and reliable, and help you produce accurate and meaningful reports that address the needs of your audience.

6.7   Cleaner production

Cleaner production (CP) is an environmental management strategy which has been widely promoted by UNEP (the United Nations Environmental Programme), focusing on preventative action during the production process through the reduction or elimination of wastes or pollutants at the source. It aims at both financial and environmental benefits, as it encourages companies to use inputs, from raw materials to energy, more productively. Cleaner production has been promoted by many governments worldwide and a significant amount of donor money has been invested in cleaner production projects in developing countries. Pollution prevention and waste minimisation initiatives in various countries have a similar focus on the prevention of pollution through source reduction options, as opposed to end of pipe abatement solutions.

CP is defined by UNEP as follows:

> Cleaner production is the continuous application of an integrated preventive environmental strategy to processes, products and services so as to increase efficiency and reduce risks to humans and the environment.
>
> For production processes, CP includes efficient use of raw materials and energy, elimination of toxic or dangerous materials, and reduction of emissions and wastes at the source. For products, the CP strategy focuses on reducing impacts along their entire life-cycle of the products and services, from design to use and ultimate disposal.

Cleaner production aims to lead to a continuous improvement process, but in many cases has struggled to make an impact beyond the low-cost options and many initial assessments have not led to major changes as the companies have not had a formal mechanism in place for pulling through environmental improvement projects with the necessary management support.

The major stages of a cleaner production process are as outlined in the flow diagram in Figure 43.

A typical CP assessment as in Figure 43 follows a similar flow as ISO14031 in respect of the selection of indicators, data collection and the use of indicators for the implementation of continual improvement programmes and the relevant tracking. The focus is on OPIs, the measurements related to the inputs and outputs. The aim is to maximise the efficiency of inputs being turned into outputs and the prevention of pollution and waste outputs. This concept is directly compatible with the graphical representation of the OPI concept in the ISO14031 standard. The economic evaluation as outlined in the feasibility stage can be applied with the support of MPIs which track costs, savings and related returns.

Figure 43 **Cleaner production assessment**

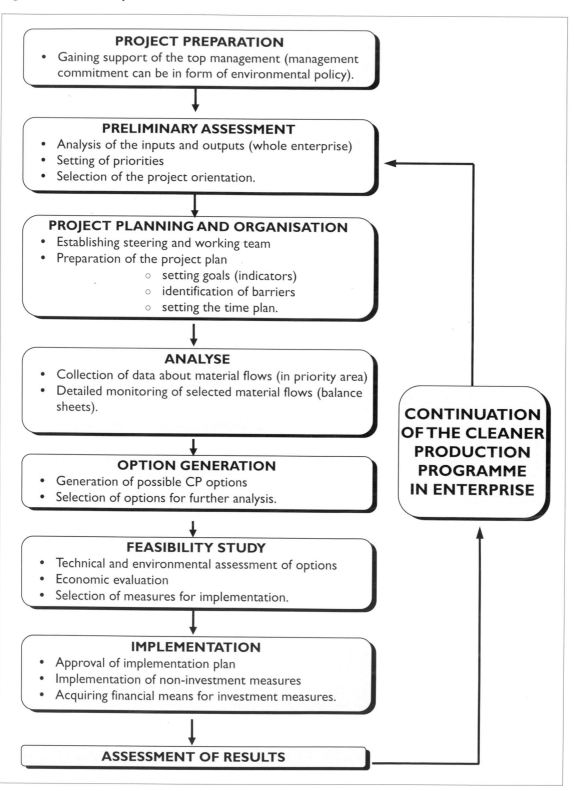

Many of the case studies in the ISO14032 technical report have used EPE as a conceptual framework for the use of CP-type implementation measures.

6.8 Using EPE and environmental performance indicators to highlight product attributes

Customers and consumers will probably account for some of the most important interested parties external to your organisation, and will provide some of the most powerful drivers for undertaking environmental activity.

Increasingly, customers and consumers are beginning to understand the impact that their purchasing decisions can have on the environment, and as this understanding grows so too do the expectations and aspirations. There is a growing trend in economies where a culture of environmental protection can be seen for customers and consumers to demand goods and services with a reduced environmental burden based on the whole life of the product, not just at the point of consumption.

In response to this, a number of schemes have been established to develop environmental standards and markings for certain products, services and industry sectors (eco-labelling). These schemes have met with varying degrees of success in the marketplace, where they have not been backed by legislative requirements. It is worth noting that eco-labelling schemes do not exist in all product, service and industry sectors.

In many cases, if an organisation does not see a benefit in adopting an eco-label, then successful introduction is rare, unless backed by legislation. Very often, compliance with and registration to eco-labelling schemes will be time consuming and costly for the organisation, and where procedural requirements are over-burdensome this can quickly erode any potential benefits. The successful schemes tend to have been supported by strong economic drivers, either from a marketing perspective, or as a defensive mechanism to maintain market share and profits, or protect against public condemnation by pressure groups (which could affect the former as well, in terms of corporate image and worth).

ISO14031 can be developed to provide environmental information on products or services, and in turn can be used to support any environmental claims made. Within the framework of established eco-labelling schemes, there are requirements to measure and report on a range of environmental criteria which demonstrate that your product or service offering meets the minimum standards stipulated by the scheme. Any ISO14031 system should recognise these as significant views of interested parties (if not significant aspects and impacts, or established environmental criteria), and thus would develop supporting indicators to address the requirements of the scheme.

Beyond existing eco-labelling schemes, it is possible to identify the expectations and aspirations of your customers and consumers (in terms of product and service characteristics) as part of the process of assessing the views of interested parties. This information may well provide you with valuable insight into what information is important to these parties, and consequently you can develop your EPE system to provide this information.

It is likely that you will want to use information to gain competitive advantage or strengthen market position, or in response to competitor activity. In certain cases, comparison of the performance of your product against that of a competitor will be possible through the use of EPE information.

Case Example   Electrolux AB, Sweden: using EPE to support product environmental claims

Electrolux is a multinational manufacturer of household and commercial appliances.

Electrolux successfully applied an EPE approach when marketing its environmental range of domestic appliances, providing information to customers on energy efficiency and life expectancy of products (among other environmentally related information). This proved to be so successful that the principles were quickly extended to all of its product lines, with targets set to improve performance on these products.

(Source: ISO TR14032, 1999.)

When we look at reporting, there is a tendency to focus on traditional methods of reporting environmental performance, but the use of eco-labels, or environmental claims on product packs or service literature, for example, can also be seen as a medium for reporting performance. It is important to note here, more than for more-conventional methods of reporting, that you will need to ensure the information is accurate and can be substantiated, as legislation exists governing the use of false claims or statements in relation to marketing products and services.

Getting an external agency to verify any information communicated which makes claims about the environmental characteristics of a product or service can provide additional assurance that you will not be in breach of legislation, or incur adverse publicity. This service will be a cost to the company, but could well prevent any unwanted repercussions when the information goes to market.

Taking this a step further, a new style of eco-labelling has emerged, referred to as 'Type III' eco labelling. This approach requires the organisation to define a number of environmental criteria for the product or service, on which externally verified information will be made available. Volvo have pioneered this approach, providing information on the environmental performance and manufacturing impact of their cars (Volvo 1998). The criteria will address significant issues of concern to the customer or consumer, as well as legislative, governmental and industry standard specified information. This approach, again, can clearly be seen to be supported by the ISO14031 approach to EPE, and offers a means by which the organisation can promote its products or services on verified environmental credentials even when more formal eco-labelling schemes are not suitable or available.

The demonstration of product attributes does not have uses only in a marketing context. Some organisations could well use such information to assess the overall environmental impact of, or environmental risk posed through, a product or service. This sort of information can be used to assist management in deciding on which products or services they need to focus efforts.

In some cases, the evaluation of a product over the whole of its life (i.e. cradle–grave evaluation), including material sourcing, production, distribution, use and disposal, may be the ultimate aim. Such (life-cycle) analysis can be extremely complex, time consuming, costly and not necessarily very accurate (depending on the assumptions made and the data used). By using relative indicators which track performance over time it is possible to get a more streamlined overview of a product's impact, with the emphasis on performance trend rather than absolute, snap-shot data. ISO14031 can provide the framework for developing such indicators and also the identification of the most critical environmental impacts to be assessed.

6.9 Supply-chain management

As mentioned in the previous section, customer and consumer demands for proven environmental responsibility from suppliers is increasing as knowledge and understanding grow of the whole-life environmental impacts of products and services. Similarly, some organisations need to be concerned with the environmental impact of their customers (e.g. financial lending organisations, institutional investors and suppliers of hazardous materials). Organisations subscribing to the ISO14001 standard for environmental management systems are further required to set objectives and targets in relation to significant aspects and impacts not only over which they have control but over which they can be expected to have an influence.

In light of this, many organisations are realising the need to manage the environmental performance of the members of their supply chains, both upstream (the supply side) and downstream (the customer side), but the effective management of supply-chain members' environmental activities has proved difficult, time consuming and costly. This is compounded when, in some cases, the supply-chain members stand a number of links away in the chain.

Common problems with environmental supply-chain management initiatives tend to centre around a lack of focus and direction of programmes, and the costly and time consuming nature of conducting a good assessment of supply-chain members' environmental activities (Wathey, 1999).

An ISO14031 EPE approach to managing supply-chain members, while not removing some of the effort required to make the programme effective and beneficial for all parties, can help provide a clear focus, and relevant, reliable and tangible information upon which to base any assessment. By adopting an EPE approach to managing the supply chain, you can select indicators which you require supply-chain partners to measure and report to you on at regular intervals. These indicators will be developed with your own objectives and targets in mind as well as those of key interested parties. This can include the supply partner in question, as it is far more likely that you will gain the commitment of these partners if there is some benefit for them as well.

Information reported against environmental indicators by supply-chain partners will still require some verification, although is likely to be less resource intensive than conducting full site audits. Furthermore, the provision of information will allow you to conduct a desk-top assessment first, to identify suspect information or unexplained deviation from expected levels, thus allowing better targeting of partners for closer inspection. The information can also indicate the highest risk partners, and consequently direct you to focus greatest scrutiny on these.

In all, the use of an ISO14031 EPE systems approach in managing the environmental impacts of supply-chain partners will help you identify and focus on the purpose of the initiative, and direct activity and resources at the most important partners (from an environmental perspective). This will potentially allow you to cover more supply-chain partners effectively and efficiently. In addition to this, if indicators are developed which focus on key areas of environmental performance for the partner organisation, then it should realise benefits as well, making the overall chain stronger.

> ## Case Example   United Utilities: applying ISO14031 to manage the environmental performance of supply-chain partners
>
> *United Utilities (UU) principally provides utilities across the North West of England in the water, electricity and telecommunications sectors for commercial and domestic users.*
>
> UU increasingly recognises the importance of the impacts that its contractors and suppliers can have on the environment, and similarly recognises its responsibilities in managing these impacts down. As more functions are out-sourced by UU, so the task of upholding this responsibility increases.
>
> In view of this UU has embarked on a scheme to manage suppliers' and contractors' environmental performance through the application of ISO14031 EPE techniques. Under the scheme, UU selected a small set of indicators which addressed its key environmental concerns. The suppliers in question would then be required to collect data, apply these to predetermined indicators and report information on a regular basis to UU to enable the tracking and reporting of environmental performance.
>
> The aim of this programme is to motivate suppliers and contractors to improve environmental performance over time in key areas. Indeed, many of the indicators developed related to areas where improvement would benefit both UU and the supply-chain member. However, information collated over time, along with other indicators, could be used to make assessments of suppliers or contractors when tenders for contracts are invited.

6.10   The application of EPE in environmental accounting

Top management need to quantify their environmental performance for certain key interested parties in financial terms. Therefore it is logical that an organisation might do this using a similar collation and reporting methodology to that used to report financial performance, especially if environmental issues can be translated into bottom-line costs or savings.

In recent years, environmental management accountancy has gained in popularity as a method of managing and tracking environmental performance among a number of large organisations. In acknowledgement of this, institutions such as financiers and insurers have begun to apply environmental accountancy methodology in an attempt to quantify the financial component of environmental performance in terms of financial costs or benefits.

Managers also need to justify environmental spend and track the performance associated with specific environmental initiatives. Often in these cases environmental accounting methodology of some sort will be applied. This allows communication to be made using a language that management feels comfortable with and that reflects the business case for a particular approach in a more objective, accurate and less emotive way. This can be used further to motivate individuals involved in such initiatives, to maintain or improve their contribution to the overall environmental performance of the organisation.

In establishing indicators for use in an environmental accounting application it is valuable to try to identify benefits and opportunities as well as the more obvious costs and risks. It is also worth noting that many environmental costs and benefits are hidden by being pooled into overhead costing, or arbitrarily assigned to certain cost centres.

Environmental accounting has also had its share of problems, due to a lack of standardised methodology, and it also has the potential to be a costly and complex exercise. The EPE approach can be much less complex than traditional accounting methods, by providing a framework which is more flexible than current management accounting protocols yet able to focus in on key costs and benefits.

Indicators are developed from a broad range of environmental pressures, aspects and impacts, and will probably focus to some extent on environmentally related costs and benefits. This focus on costs and benefits when linked to the commitment to continual improvement should lead to the identification of potential cost savings.

Appendix 1 Brainstorming key environmental issues, pressures and aspirations

Issues and Pressures	Rating	Value of ISO14031	Potential Benefits	Rating	Notes
Quality of water discharged to sewer to be within specified limits.		Data monitored at regular intervals can help identify adverse trends or abnormal conditions.	Reduced risk of breaching the terms of the consent to discharge to sewer, and thus of facing prosecution and fines.		
Contractual requirement for packaging to contain a minimum of 80% recycled material.		Indicators can be established to track the percentage of recycled material used in packaging for a specific contract.	Reduced risk of breaching contract and incurring penalty charges and product returns from customer.		
Adverse publicity relating to the sourcing of components from suppliers prosecuted for pollution incidents.		Indicators can be established for suppliers to report against, with criteria established for pollution incidents.	Increases pressure on suppliers to improve environmental management, allows incidents to be highlighted and tracked, and risk to be assessed.		
Increases in production costs due to the rising cost of fuel oil.		Indicators can be established for fuel usage, and data collected on fuel costs.	Will help identify areas for fuel efficiency initiatives, and provide real cost data by production unit.		

Organisational Aspirations	Rating	Value of ISO14031	Potential Benefits	Rating	Notes
Compliance with government voluntary initiatives on CO$_2$ reporting.		Indicators can be established to produce CO$_2$ emission information as required under government guidelines.	Raises the profile of the organisation as an environmentally responsible body, pre-empts enforced reporting and provides information on sources for further reduction initiatives.		
Initiation of local community conservation projects.		Indicators can track involvement in project and the response of local communities.	Helps build relationships with local communities, increases positive publicity and provides information for external environmental reporting.		
Continual improvement in environmental performance.		Indicators can track progress against all key areas of environmental performance.	Benefits from continual improvement in meeting ISO14001 policy commitments, helps build reputation and credibility of the organisation.		

Appendix 2   Outline planning template

Tasks	By Whom	Calendar e.g. Days, Weeks, Months, periods, Shift rotations													Cost	Notes
Secure initial top management commitment																
Establish the core EPE team																
Review relevant environmental legislation and regulations																
Identify organisational environmental performance criteria																
Assess the views of interested parties																
Evaluate environmental costs and benefits																
Identify significant aspects and impacts																
Assess existing practices and procedures																
Appraise the features of the organisation (structure, culture, barriers and opportunities)																
Develop goals and direction for the EPE system																
Revise plan for presentation to top management in order to gain further commitment																
Select indicators																
Plan implementation and ongoing operation																
Gain final approval and commitment																
Implement EPE programme																
Review EPE project after six months																

Key		
Use to identify any symbols, colours, code numbers, typefaces or abbreviations	Italics indicate example text	*abc*

Appendix 3   Resource identification record

Task	Resource (Labour, Training, Specialists, Facilities, Support, Contingency)	Quantity of Resource	Total Cost of Resource	Notes

Appendix 4   Skills and knowledge requirements matrix

| Project Team | Central Environmental Management | | | | | | Updated on | 31.1.00 | | |
Team Member's Name	Position in Team (if specified)	Required Skills or Knowledge	Y/N	Sc	RT	FT	Date Trained	Notes	Pr
A.N. Example	Deputy Team Head	Environmental awareness	Y	7	N	N	21.2.99	No action	
		Knowledge of ISO14001	Y	4	Y	N	14.6.99	Awareness-raising session required only	
		Understanding of ISO14031	N	–	N	Y	–	Full programme	
		Training skills	Y	8	N	N	21.6.95	No action	
		Auditing qualification	Y	2	N	Y	5.9.98	No auditing since qualification. Full programme, not urgent	
		Presentation skills	Y	6	N	N	21.6.95	No action	

Key

Y/N   Currently possesses skill or knowledge, yes or no

Sc   Competency score for skill or knowledge (1–10, 1 = low, 10 = high)

RT   Requires refresher training

FT   Requires full training

Pr   Priority rating for actions identified

Appendix 5 Training and knowledge-building planning chart

DATE:

Training or knowledge-building activity	Team member/ delegate	Date completed satisfactorily	Calendar e.g. Days, Weeks, Months, Periods, Shift rotations.					Cost	Hours Duration	Notes

Key:

Activity planned	
Activity completed, satisfactorily	
Activity completed, unsatisfactorily	
Activity postponed	
Activity overdue	
Activity cancelled	
Activity rescheduled	
Delegate withdrawn	
Delegate absent	

Appendix 6 Record of the organisation's environmental performance criteria

Details of the environmental criteria applied within the organisation	At what level is the criteria applied within the organisation?	Priority rating	Is it actively applied?	Is it relevant or desired?	Notes

Key for priority rating:

Appendix 7   Record of the views of interested parties

Name of Interested Party (3.1.3.1)	Significance Rating (3.1.3.3)	View of Interested Parties Annotate [L] = Likely, [C] = Communicated (3.1.3.2 & 3.1.3.5)	Significance Rating (3.1.3.4)	Further Notes

Appendix 8   Environmental cost and benefit identification matrix

Reference	Cost / Benefit Type	Current	Est. Value	Potential	Est. Value	Notes
Examples: Cost of waste disposal per annum	C	General waste skips uplift, and landfill charges (excluding tax).	Cost £25,000	Charges set to rise with closure of three landfill sites in area over the next two years.	£28,750	Estimated rise of 15% over two years without inflation.
Reduction of waste through segregating recyclable materials	S	Trial segregation project suggests potential to reduce costs by 20%.	Saved £500	Capital equipment to implement segregation across operation, estimated cost in year one £3500. Staff training approx. £500.	Saving: £5000 pa now. £5750 pa year 2.	Year 1 saving less £4000 costs. Saving now based on current costs. Saving Year 2 based on projected costs.
Cost of auditing waste-handling contractors	X	Audit costs and expenses per annum	£600	Likely cost of prosecution under duty of care legislation	£30,000	Fines, legal costs and remedial action Does not include damage to reputation or lost business.

Key to cost/benefit types	
C	Cost
S	Saving
R	Revenue
X	Risk
P	Perception
Q	Qualitative

Appendix 9 Aspect and impact brainstorming checklist

Activity / Product / Service			
Aspect / Impact	**Rating**	**Notes**	**Likely Significance**
Emissions to Air;			
Greenhouse Gasses			
Acidifying Gasses			
Ozone Depleters			
Particulate Matter			
Air Quality Reduction			
VOC's			
Discharges to Water;			
Dangerous Substances			
Slurry			
BOD/COD			
Eutrophication			
Total Suspended Solids			
Disposal on Land;			
General Waste			
Special Waste			
Contamination Issues			
Statutory Nuisance			
Noiseand/or Vibration			
Odours			
Littering			
Dust and Smoke			
Traffic			
Light Pollution			
Human Health			
Toxicity (Short Term/Persistent)			
Allergenic and Sensitising			
Radioactive			
Infectious			
Physical Hazard			
Ecological			
Habitat Destruction			
Reduction of Bio-Diversity			
Visual Intrusion			
Land Use/Disruption			
Consumption			
Resource Depletion			
Water			
Energy			
Product Attributes			
Transport			
Packaging Waste			
Recycled Content versus Virgin			
Potential for Re-Use			
Recoverability			
Service Extension/Longevity			

Key to Rating

✓ = important

* = very important

? = more information required

Appendix 10   Register of aspects and impacts by activity, product or service

Activity / Product / Service *			
Aspect	Impact	Significance	Notes

* Delete as appropriate

Appendix 11   Evaluation record for existing practices and procedures

Practice or procedure	Issues pressure, aspect or impact	What data is available?	R, X or D	When collected?	How much historical data?	Who owns the data?	Further notes	Relevance	Reliability
Water-meter reading	Water consumption (Aspect)	Water usage for whole site	R	Weekly	18 months	Facilities management	Data is communicated to environment dept. weekly for collation of performance reports	High	High

Key R   Routinely, data are recorded and provided on a regular basis, according to predetermined timescales.

X   By exception, data are monitored regularly but only reported if outside predetermined parameters.

D   On demand, data can be obtained but are only provided if demanded.

Appendix 12　Organisational structure evaluation template

Variable in organisational Structure	Current (and/or foreseeable) situation	Foreseeable impacts on EPE system development
Product or service orientated		
Number of sites or operating locations, subdivisions or functions		
Range of activities and technologies		
Labour or capital intensive		
Stability of workforce		
Clarity of responsibilities and nature of reporting lines		
Nature of reporting structure and communication lines		
Flexibility for change		
Formal or informal		
Centralised or decentralised		

Appendix 13   Organisational culture evaluation template

Variable in organisational culture	Current (and/or foreseeable) situation	Foreseeable impacts on EPE system development
Management focus, i.e. sales, production, marketing		
Proactive or reactive		
Open or reserved		
Importance of traditions and history		
Level of autonomy or empowerment		
Relationships between management and staff		
Relationships between managers		
Extent to which people are target orientated and have commitment to achieving agreed levels of performance		
Attitudes towards innovation		
Attitudes towards costs		
Attitudes towards investment		
Level of commitment and loyalty of staff to the organisation		
Elitism or tolerant development		
Attitudes towards risk		

Appendix 14 Environmental goal setting matrix

Primary Focus	Secondary Focus	Category	Goals (aspirations and expectations)	Barriers	Opportunities

Key to category abbreviations

A/I = Aspect or impact
L/V = Legal or voluntary requirement
PC = Organisational performance criteria
IP = View of interested party or parties
C/B = Cost or benefit

Appendix 15   Summary of goals and outline plans

Goals	Outline Plans for Achieving Goals

Appendix 16 Identifying broad environmental topics, interested parties and indicators

Broad Environmental Topic	Interested Parties	Indicator Information Requirements	Potential Indicator	Notes

Appendix 17 Indicator profile recording template

Indicator Reference	Set		Indicator			
Indicator Details						
Topic Area						
Interested Parties						
Intended Purpose						
Data Required	Timing	Location	Scope	Unit	Reference	Type
	Data Source					
	Data Source					
ISO14031 Description						
Category			Characteristic			
Additional Notes						
Detail of Required Actions						
Resources Required						
Barriers			Opportunities			
Required Data Collection and Communication Procedures						
Required Data Collection and Communication Procedures						

Appendix 18   Summary of indicators

Topic	Indicator Set	Indicator Detail	Reference	Indicator Detail	Reference	Indicator Detail	Reference	Indicator Detail	Reference

Appendix 19 Review process structure

Level				Review Name	Timing	Scope	Notes
1				Group EPE and EMS meeting	Half Yearly week 4		
	a			Group EPE action forum	Quarterly week 2		
2				West region EPE action forum	Monthly week 1		
3	a	1		West region green team sales	Monthly week 4		
	a	1	a	West region green team account management	Monthly week 4		
4	a	1	b	East region EPE action forum	Monthly week 1		
3	a	2		East region green team sales	Monthly week 4		
	a	2	a	East region green team account management	Monthly week 4		
4	a	2	b	Overseas EPE action forum	Monthly week 1		
3	a	3		Overseas green team sales operations	Monthly week 1		
4	a	3	a				

Appendix 20　Activity and attendee summary

Activity	Attendee Name (or group)	Duration	Location	Notes	Date Completed	Attendee Signature
Initial project awareness bulletin	All company employees All temporary and agency staff Maintenance contractors on site	1 week (posters 3 weeks lead-time)	All company	Memo to all staff, posters for notice boards, and inclusion in weekly brief.		See departmental records attached.

Appendix 21   Initiation plan schedule

Activity	Duration	Location	Booked	Closed	Numbers	Cost	Notes

Calendar   e.g. Days, Weeks, Months, Periods, Shift rotations.

Key:

Appendix 22 Feedback summary record

Activity	Date	Summary of Feedback	Required Action	By Whom	Proposed Date	Scheduled	Completed
Data-collection training for vehicle maintenance section.	31.7.00	Pro forma for recording consumption of lubricants duplicates recording on job cards.	Review data-collection process to obtain data on lubricant usage from job-card summaries prepared by workshop office.	EPE manager and workshop supervisor	11.8.00	Y	10.8.00

Appendix 23   Review specification

Review Name			Reference	
Timing		Location/facility		
Scope				
Format				
Review Leader		Minute Taker		
Attendees				
Feeder Reviews		Input from		
Receiving Reviews		Output to		
Associated Reports (if applicable)		Report Timings (can affect review scheduling)		
Feedback Mechanism(s)				
Further Notes				

Glossary

Continual improvement: 'Process of enhancing the environmental management system to achieve improvements in overall environmental performance in line with the organisation's environmental policy' (ISO14001, 1996). (The process need not take place in all areas of activity simultaneously.)

Environment: 'Surroundings in which an organisation operates including air, water, land, natural resources, flora, fauna, humans and their interrelation' (ISO14001, 1996). (Surroundings in this context extend from within an organisation to the global system.)

Environmental aspect: 'Element of an organisation's activities, products or services that can interact with the environment' (ISO14001, 1996). (A significant environmental aspect is an environmental aspect that has or can have a significant environmental impact.)

Environmental condition indicator (ECI): 'Specific expression that provides information about the local, regional, national, or global condition of the environment' (ISO14031, 1999). (An ECI is not a measure of impacts on the environment. 'Regional' may refer to a state, a province, or a group of states within a country, or it may refer to a group of countries or a continent, depending on the scale of the condition of the environment that the organisation chooses to consider.)

Environmental impact: 'Any change to the environment, whether adverse or beneficial, wholly or partially resulting from an organisation's activities, products or services' (ISO14031, 1999).

Environmental management system (EMS): 'An environmental management system is the part of the overall management system that includes organisational structure, planning activities, responsibilities, practices, procedures, processes and resources for developing, implementing, achieving, reviewing and maintaining the environmental policy' (ISO14001, 1996; ISO14031, 1999).

Environmental objective: 'Overall environmental goal, arising from the environmental policy that an organisation sets itself to achieve, and which is quantified where practicable' (ISO14031, 1999).

Environmental performance: 'Measurable results of the environmental management system, related to an organisation's control of its environmental aspects, based on its environmental policy, objectives and targets' (ISO14001, 1996); 'Results of an organisation's management of its environmental aspects' (ISO14031, 1999). (In the context of environmental management systems, results may be measured against the organisation's environmental policy, objectives and targets.)

Environmental performance criterion: 'Environmental objective, target, or other intended level of environmental performance set by the management of the organisation and used for the purpose of environmental performance evaluation' (ISO14031, 1999).

Environmental performance evaluation (EPE): 'Process to facilitate management decisions regarding an organisation's environmental performance by selecting indicators, collecting and analysing data, assessing information against environmental performance criteria, reporting and communicating, and periodically reviewing and improving of this process' (ISO14031, 1999).

Environmental performance indicator (EPI): 'Specific expression that provides information about an organisation's environmental performance' (ISO14031, 1999).

Environmental policy: 'Statement by the organisation of its intentions and principles in relation to its overall environmental performance which provides a framework for action and for the setting of its environmental objectives and targets' (ISO14031, 1999).

Environmental target: 'Detailed performance requirement, quantified where practicable, applicable to the organisation or parts thereof, that arises from the environmental objectives and that needs to be set and met in order to achieve those objectives' (ISO14031, 1999).

Interested parties: 'Individual or group concerned with or affected by the environmental performance of the organisation' (ISO14001, 1996).

Management performance indicator (MPI): 'Environmental performance indicator that provides information about the management efforts to influence an organisation's environmental performance' (ISO14031, 1999).

Operational performance indicator (OPI): 'Environmental performance indicator that provides information about the environmental performance of an organisation's operations' (ISO14031, 1999).

List of References

14000 & ONE Solutions (2000). *DTI: ISO14031 Demonstration project: Phase one project report* (Bolton: 14000 & ONE Solutions).

Business in the Environment (BiE) (2000). www.business-in-environment.org.uk

ICI (1997). *Environmental burden: The ICI approach* (ICI).

ISO (International Organisation for Standardisation) (1996). *ISO14001: Environmental management systems: Specification with guidance for use* (Geneva: ISO).

ISO (International Organisation for Standardisation) (1996). *ISO14004: Environmental management systems: General guidance on principles, systems and supporting techniques* (Geneva: ISO).

ISO (International Organisation for Standardisation) (1999). *ISO14031: Environmental management: Environmental performance evaluation: Guidelines* (Geneva: ISO).

ISO (International Organisation for Standardisation) (1999). *ISO14032: Environmental management: Examples of environmental performance evaluation (EPE).*

Volvo Car Corporation (1998). *Environmental Product Declaration: S80 1999* (Sweden: Volvo).

Wathey, D. (1999). *Developing environmental supply chain management programmes: A practical case study* (MSc Thesis, University of Bradford).

Further Reading

Azzone, G. and Manzini, R., 'Measuring strategic environmental performance', *Business Strategy and the Environment*, vol. 3, no. 1 (1994), pp.1–14.

Bennett, M. and James, P., *Environment under the spotlight: Current practice and future trends in environmental-related performance measurement for business* (London: Certified Accountants Educational Trust, 1998).

Bennett, M. and James, P., 'ISO14031 and the future of EPE', in M. Bennett. and P. James, *Sustainable measures: Evaluation and reporting of environmental and social performance* (Sheffield: Greenleaf Publishing Ltd), pp. 76–97.

Bennett, M. and James, P., *Sustainable measures: Evaluation and reporting of environmental and social performance* (Sheffield: Greenleaf Publishing Ltd, 1999).

Bragg, S., Knapp, P. and McLean, R., *Improving environmental performance: A guide to a proven and effective approach* (Letchworth, UK: Technical Communications, 1993).

Business in the Environment (BiE), *A measure of commitment: Guidelines for measuring environmental performance* (London: Business in the Environment and KPMG Peat Marwick, 1992).

CIRIA (Construction Industries Research and Information Association), *Environmental management in construction* (London: CIRIA, 2000).

Department of the Environment, *Indicators for sustainable development for the United Kingdom* (London: HMSO, 1996).

Department of the Environment, Transport and the Regions, *Take up the challenge: Make a corporate commitment, MACC2* (London: HMSO, 2000).

Ditz, D. and Ranganathan, J., *Measuring up: Towards a common framework for tracking environmental performance* (Washington, DC: World Resources Institute, 1997).

Epstein, M., *Measuring corporate environmental performance: Best practices for costing and managing an effective environmental strategy* (New York: Irwin, 1996).

European Green Table, *Environmental performance indicators in industry. Report 5: Practical experiences with developing EPIs with 12 companies* (Oslo Norwegian Confederation of Business and Industry, 1997).

Federal Environment Ministry, Germany, *A guide to corporate environmental indicators* (Bonn & Berlin: Federal Environment Ministry, 1997).

Global Reporting Initiative, *Sustainability reporting guidelines: Exposure draft for public comment in pilot testing* (Boston, MA: CERES, 1999).

ISO (International Organisation for Standardisation), *ISO14010: Guidelines for environmental auditing: General principles* (Geneva: ISO, 1996).

ISO (International Organisation for Standardisation), *ISO14011: Guidelines for environmental auditing: Audit procedures: Auditing of environmental management systems* (Geneva: ISO, 1996).

ISO (International Organisation for Standardisation), *ISO14050: Environmental management: Vocabulary* (Geneva: ISO, 1998).

Jones, K., Alabaster, T. and Walton, J., 'Virtual environments in environmental reporting', *Greener Management International,* Issue 21, Spring 1998, pp. 121–135.

Keffer, C., Shimp, R. and Lehni, M., *Eco-efficiency indicators and reporting: Report on the status of the project's work in progress and guideline for pilot application* (Geneva: WBCSD, 1999).

Kuhre, W., *ISO14031: Environmental performance evaluation (EPE)* (New Jersey: Prentice-Hall PTR, 1998).

Sammut, A., *Measuring Environmental performance: An analysis of environmental performance indicators in the water industry* (MSc Thesis, University of Bradford, 1999).

SustainAbility and UNEP (United Nations Environmental Programme), *Engaging stakeholders. The 1997 Benchmark Survey* (London: SustainAbility/UNEP, 1996).

SustainAbility and UNEP (United Nations Environmental Programme), *Engaging stakeholders. I. The benchmark survey: The second international progress report on company environmental reporting* (Paris: UNEP; London: SustainAbility, 1996).

Water UK Sustainability Group, United Kingdom Water Industry Research Ltd., Environmental Resources Management Ltd, and Environmental Resolve, *Towards a set of environmental sustainability indicators for the UK water industry: Paper for discussion with external stakeholders* (London: Water UK, 1999).

Index